Dreamland
The Story of an Earth Angel

Written by Melina Mortensen

Copyright © 2022 Melina Mortensen

All rights reserved. No part of this publication may be reproduced, distributed, or transmitted in any form or by any means, including photocopying, recording, or other electronic or mechanical methods, without the prior written permission of the publisher, except in the case of brief quotations embodied in critical reviews and certain other noncommercial uses permitted by copyright law. For permission requests, write the author @ pleiadianstarmother@gmail.com attention: Permissions

ISBN: (Paperback) 978-0880-0877-5

Cover Design: Austin Foster

Cover Design Images: https://www.dreamstime.com/brain-science-intelligence-genius-education-concept-smart-head-profile-space-inside-future-ai-element-image-image219339461

https://www.shutterstock.com/image-illustration/darkhaired-girl-angel-wings-goes-sun-1036348708

Edited By: Diana Henderson, Creative Type and Realization Press

To all the benevolent beings in my life both seen and unseen who remind me I am a child of The Creator and guide me through the challenges and joys I experience on Earth

Foreword

So many people are "seeking." We seek purpose, answers, guidance, help, connection, happiness, psychic awareness, the meaning of it all. We seek to understand what lies beyond the world we see with our physical eyes. There is a part of our soul that knows that there is something more…something inherently intangible yet profoundly palpable waiting behind the curtain to invite us into a grand secret. Like planning a surprise party for a friend just so you can share in the joy of their surprise and show them how much they mean to you.

When one joins the seeker's path, the Universe performs a delightful symphony of synchronistic convergences in celebration, bringing that seeker Divine guidance and messages in a way they can receive in order to grow toward the realization of their true self. In the spiritual and energetic world, the dream state is both the simplest and most complex symphony to play.

All spiritual beings having a human experience dream. Not only is it scientifically a necessary part of our survival, but it is also a gateway into our self-awareness, a front row seat into our heart and soul spaces where our truest desires can be explored. As we rest our bodies nightly and enter this magical place, where limitations are nonexistent, we can play out what is possible and even dabble in the potential to rewrite the past in favor of a new outcome.

This also happens to be a space where our Divine connections, our angels and guides, the energy of our soul, can speak to us, unhindered by the trappings of our day-to-day monkey mind musings. In this state, we are wide open and boundaryless. We get out of our own way to receive the improbable, the impossible, and embrace what *can* be.

Yet dreams can be tricky. They do not always provide obvious or straightforward information. Environments and faces peppered with confusing symbols and spaces, nonsensical timelines, and often overwhelming emotional moments can be difficult to interpret. How does one extrapolate meaning and make sense of their dreaming mind? How can one discern between a basic dream and one of *those dreams* where there is a message to decipher and apply? And taking it a step further, when one does experience a dream that offers great detail, a message, and a strong urge to "do something" with it, what can be done?

Melina Mortensen is no stranger to these very questions. *Dreamland* is a fascinating dive into one seeker's dreams and the possibilities they hold for those wishing to "be the change." Learning the often complicated and always significant world of dreams while hopping from scene to scene in her psychic "super cape," Melina is an inspiration to all dreamers and seekers looking to make sense of and take meaning from their visions.

Yes, one person can make a difference.

She is redefining the phrase, "It's just a dream," and empowering others to discover intentional communication from the spiritual realm to the physical one.

In *Dreamland*, a seeker who dreams can find meaning in Melina's story and perhaps even relate to the personal adversity many on this path face in finding themselves.

We all work in our own unique ways intuitively. This journey is a wonderful read for those working out how they "tick," those with a curiosity or fascination with the dream world and how it can aid us in the waking state, and those on "the seeker's path" looking for answers, clues even, to the "why" of it all.

So, get comfy, grab a warm drink or a glass of wine, and get ready to enter a world of life-changing dreams. You never know how they will inspire your journey.

With love and gratitude,
Stacey
The Black Feather Intuitive

Acknowledgments

I would like to express my heartfelt gratitude to my mentor, The Black Feather Intuitive, who has been invaluable to my awakening and has helped me enormously to fully understand who I am and my capabilities with the gifts The Creator has given me. I don't know that I will ever be able to express to her just how much her mentoring means to me. She is rock solid and a beautiful soul who has given so much to so many people over the years. Surely, God has blessed me with her presence in my life, and I pray she has a full understanding of the glory she brings to the world.

I extend my love and appreciation to my "mother from another lifetime," my therapist, Rachel Hensley, for helping me to see the potential in myself.

Much love and appreciation to my daughter, Mekenna Mortensen, my beloved sons, Kristian Mortensen and Simon Mortensen, and to my mom, Karen Foster Montgomery, my stepfather, Ralph Montgomery, and to Erik Mortensen, the father of my beautiful children, for all the love and support you have shown me.

And to my editor, Diana Henderson, thank you for gracefully refining the book to become a piece of work I can be proud of.

"Our deepest fear is not that we are inadequate. Our deepest fear is that we are powerful beyond measure. It is our light, not our darkness that most frightens us. We ask ourselves, 'Who am I to be brilliant, gorgeous, talented, and fabulous?' Actually, who are you not to be? You are a child of God. Your playing small does not serve the world. There's nothing enlightening about shrinking, so that other people won't feel insecure around you. We are all meant to shine, as children do. We were born to make manifest the glory of God that is within us. It's not just in some of us; it's in everyone and as we let our own light shine, we unconsciously give other people permission to do the same. As we are liberated from our own fear our presence automatically liberates others."

Marianne Williamson, *A Return to Love* (1992)

Introduction

I have had vivid dreams all my life. I can recall an innate fear of the bedtime hour as young as two years old. I still have misgivings every night just before closing my eyes. The difference now is I know I'm not alone. Beside me every step of the way are benevolent beings I have known since I first sparked off from the divine. They walk beside me to assist in my "nightwork" as well as guide me on an unpaved path in a unique existence.

Recently, during a channeling from my psychic mentor whom I have been working with since the fall of 2020, my benevolent helpers advised, "Be at peace, dear one. We are honored to be connecting with you today. We would like to acknowledge the great effort that you have taken and the great listening you have done in such a short period of time on Earth.... Do not be afraid to continue to take small steps. The small steps are necessary at this time to build the foundation and the pathway, and your pathway is not a solid piece of cement. It is made of building blocks and interlocking bricks that come into the mix to weave multiple energies to strengthen the path ahead. This path has never been walked before by you or any other. Remove your idea of what is supposed to be, what is supposed to come about. It has already been determined and decided—by you. You must trust that this is what is unfolding now. Focus on your moment, not the past and not the future. We understand the irony of this statement as you do much in timelines within the dream state. We leave you with this information now to ponder, and we are honored to have had this time. We step back now with much love."

Over these past months, I have learned that what I thought were just "dreams" were in fact out-of-body experiences, traveling dimensional timelines with the mission of cleaning up karma. Each time I step outside of my body and move to other timelines, I am presented with an opportunity for an altered outcome. In most cases, my presence in that slice of time prevents the death of a victim, alters the karma for a perpetrator who would have carried out a transgression against another living soul, or otherwise paints a new timeline in which the outcome is quite different from the one that previously existed.

What I present in the following pages is a glimpse into my awakening and subsequent dreamwork to offer a firsthand account of what my time traveling experiences "look like." I invite readers to have a movie seat to "watch" exactly what it is I do at night. I also share accounts of previous lives and glimpses of spiritual beings that have worked with me in the past or are yet to appear in my current lifetime. We hear from Source, who, prior to my awakening, I believed to be unreachable. Source for me was "out there somewhere," just watching and not really being present in my life. I've learned just how wrong I was and just how much I had been conditioned into believing that Source was a bystander as I fumbled through life trying to understand who I was and why I was here on Earth.

I welcome you to walk with me into *Dreamland* and witness what time traveling experiences are like for an Earth angel, which is what I have learned I am. I am here, along with millions of other starseeds, to help the world, to assist humanity, and to advise based on lifetimes of gathered wisdom. What follows is my personal account, but it is not meant just for me. This is perhaps an activation for other still sleeping starseeds or an opportunity for a fresh perspective on how benevolent guidance is offered. I invite you to be open to receiving what I have to offer in these pages. Please remain receptive as you peer inside my "dreams." You may just come out on the other side wide awake.

Chapter One
Betty White

I see Betty White. She is looking right at me. "Wait a minute," I say to myself. "She just passed three days ago." But there she is smiling her contagious smile.

As I gazed at her, she slowly began to change. She initially appeared to be 99 years old, but, as I continued watching, I saw her face transform. Just seconds later, Betty White was back to being 30 years old! Her face was young, and her hair was now a luxurious brown. Her smile remained bright, and she was very pleased with herself. My eyes shot open, and I found I was smiling as well. Wow! I loved being able to see the dead at least when I was viewing them like this.

I had been fighting myself most of my life. I never really understood the "love yourself" mantra until I was fifty-three. I didn't even know what loving yourself meant. It was the summer of 2020, and I had recently left my husband of thirteen years. I had started sessions with a therapist in an attempt to put everything into perspective and get out from underneath the tractor I felt had just run over me.

Everything about leaving him felt right, and I loved the new apartment I had moved into with my beloved dog, Larry. However, getting out from underneath all the baggage was another ballgame altogether. This was lifetimes of baggage, and I understood that on a soul level. In my heart, I realized that I "knew" my husband before this lifetime. Something was oddly familiar about him, the relationship itself, and the way it ended. I just couldn't put my finger on what.

At a session one afternoon, my therapist said, "You have to love yourself first, and I believe your ex is a karmic relationship for you."

I looked at her quizzically and asked, "Love myself? What does that even mean?" Followed by, "Karmic relationship? What do you mean there?"

I was under the impression that karma was some type of bad behavior a person carried out either in this lifetime or another that eventually came back to haunt them. Somehow, there was a debt to be paid. My therapist went on to explain that karmic meant "something to learn" and that my husband was here to teach me about some aspect of myself. There was a grand lesson to be had by the whole experience.

Walking outside after the session into the blinding sun and oven-like heat, I got in my car, turned the air conditioner on high, and searched "karmic relationship" on my cell phone. From that moment on, it seemed as if my life was on fast forward. Actually, stop and rewind. I know the moment it went to fast forward. It was the day before this meeting with my therapist.

Chapter Two
Jesus and Mary

I was sitting in my living room watching TV that hot afternoon, wondering where I was supposed to go from here—now that I was free from a turbulent thirteen-year relationship that involved everything from drug and alcohol abuse to verbal, emotional, and physical abuse. I sat pondering what my next move would be and how I could rebound into a healthy, happy life. I would be remiss if I pretended that it was all my ex because I was in it up to my knees.

We had fallen into a routine years before of drinking every night. It was the way we "spent time together" and, try as we did to come off normal by day, the drugs and drinking were there every night. That was how we existed together. After a decade of this behavior, however, I could not do it any longer and, just like that, in the summer of 2019, I got sober. No more drugs, no more alcohol. I went to bed at a normal time just like the rest of the world. I knew deep in my bones this would bring about the rapid decline of what remained of us as a couple, and, by the summer of 2020, I was gone.

So, on the couch crying to the point of being sick to my stomach, I ran into my closet where I kept a small shrine to Jesus and Mary, who had been by my side most of my life but on whom I rarely called. I got on my knees and unloaded. Praying and screaming that it was all too much. That what was happening to me was too much to bear alone. Begging for help, I went on and on until, exhausted, I climbed out of the closet. The following day was the first meeting with my therapist.

Chapter Three
The Soul Contract

Let's go back to the hot car and the karmic research I was doing. I sat in the car for about forty-five minutes with the air conditioner running as I read article after article about how souls incarnate together either to teach us something or for us to teach them something or both of us having something to learn from the other. I looked up from my phone after seeing the time and realized just how long I had been sitting outside of her office. I put the car in drive and headed home to do more research on the computer.

As I drove home, I had this overwhelming feeling that this lifetime would be my last. I just knew it. So much so that I said it out loud, "This is it for me. This is the end of the story. My final chapter." I spent hours that night clicking around on the internet searching for more information about souls who incarnated together and karmic relationships. It felt as if my fingers were being guided to certain articles to read and research. Finally, exhausted, I shut the computer down and went to bed.

The next morning, I woke up and had breakfast, took my dog Larry on a walk, and, after he settled into his chair, I felt a compulsion to get on the internet again. I had a relentless urge I could not ignore to contact a psychic to see if I could get clarification on my karmic relationship with my husband. Again, the automatic clicking began and before I knew it, I was making my first online appointment with a psychic set just a couple of days later.

The morning of the internet session, I was again crying over the end of my relationship and was desperate for answers. The screen came up and there she was. Right away she looked deeply concerned as I was crying and saying, "Who is he? Who is he?" She asked if this was my first time to contact a psychic, and I told her it was. She looked surprised but proceeded right away to get to the question I kept repeating.

Her eyes opened and she said, "Soul contract. You signed a soul contract with him. This is your fifth lifetime together. Your first lifetime was as his brother. You both were the sons of a priest who ran the temple and ranked high in the tribe. He was hard on both of you. Putting you into a cave without water or provisions. He wanted his sons to fend for themselves and learn to be men. I can see you both fighting the elements and wildlife to stay alive. Later, I see each of you participating in human sacrifices. It is part of your role in the temple and the expectations of your father. The other three lifetimes I see you are his wife. One time is the medieval ages. He is the best-looking man in the village and could have had any woman he wanted but he picked you. Then I see you in *Little House on the Prairie* type clothes and period. You are waiting at the edge of the woods for him to come out. He is a logger of some sort and stays away for weeks at a time. When he does come home, he gives you scraps of affection. You die that lifetime. You stop eating and sleeping and basically wither away while he is gone. Now is your fifth lifetime together, and this time you have chosen yourself."

She went on to say, "You signed the contract with him, not him with you. You were there when he was making his blueprint for this life, and he was looking for someone to show him unconditional love. You raised your hand, signed the contract, and that is what you have done. In fact, you were done with that contract years ago!"

Though I knew in my heart that what she was saying was true and it all fell into place comfortably for me, I still couldn't believe my ears. I sat in front of the computer just staring back at her when finally, I said, "I knew it! I knew he was familiar!"

Yes, this time I had chosen myself just as she had said.

She added, "He also showed you something. He showed you how to stand up and be strong."

I was incredulous and denied he had shown me anything. I was still in the throes of my grief and anger and wasn't ready to give him credit. We went on to discuss a few other topics I don't remember, and after hanging up I went and lay on my bed to take in all that she had told me.

This is where it all began, or did it start months before? Leading up to my leaving my ex-husband for good, I made four trips to my parents' house in Houston, Texas, to spend a few days to just over a week. These trips came when he and I argued and there were no more drugs or alcohol to cover up the pain. One evening sitting on my mother's couch, I looked at her. Feeling tired, I said, "Mom, I'm old. I mean really, really old. I feel like I'm thousands of years old."

She looked at me questioningly and asked, "What are you talking about?"

I replied, "I don't exactly know, Mom. It's just something I'm sure of."

Chapter Four
Out of Place

As a young girl, I felt out of place, and I don't mean the kind of awkwardness most of us feel while in school. It was like the whole Earth was not my natural home but somewhere I was for the time being. I could always sense I was separate from everyone else. I was an observer of sorts, constantly gauging, measuring, and sizing up the people I met. I could be sitting on a city bus, inside a grocery store, or at a crowded restaurant, and my senses would be on overload. I felt like I had an invisible radar device and could scan my environment, stopping at each person and getting a feel for who they were. I would sit and stare and could sense their stories unfolding right in front of me. However, it was more than that. I could also feel what they were feeling, almost read their thoughts.

There was something just under the surface that set me apart, but I didn't know what. This internal scanning talent measured any situation I was in. Even at a young age, I could feel the difference between myself and others. Somehow, I wasn't at the same vibration as those around me. Whether it was walking to school alone (my mother at work already) at the age of six to start the first grade and knowing what was ahead of me in childhood or sitting in the classroom, I would observe the other children, the teacher, and my environment to discern what was acceptable behavior and how I could best fit in. That first day of the first grade remains clear as a bell even now.

My six-year-old self walked up to the red building. I could see a teacher with a beehive hairdo and purple suit on; her name was Mrs. Rogers, and during the school year I would develop a bond with her as I did with almost every teacher I had all the way through college. I was good at making friends with the teachers rather than the students.

This came so naturally to me that I basically didn't have many friends growing up that were my age. Those I did try to make friends with were, for the most part, insincere. By the time I was in fourth grade, I began acting out, although not in class. If someone tried to show an interest in becoming my friend, I would say something rude so the friendship would not develop. Even with a few boys who wanted to go steady, I would yell and lash out towards them. (I even gave a sweet young boy a bloody nose for trying to kiss me one day after school!) That way, I wouldn't be disappointed when the relationship went south. I retreated more and more into myself and my separateness.

In fifth grade, the bullying started. *Maybe,* I thought, *this is payback for the kids I was rude to the year before.* One girl had it out for me and threatened me physically almost every day. This was back in the 1970s when bully prevention was not even heard of. If I told on her, I felt it would only make the bullying worse, so I suffered in silence and laid low and tried to stay out of her way.

The separateness only got worse in middle school. When I got off the city bus and saw the children in front of the school waiting for the homeroom bell, I walked slowly and in a wide circle, trying to pass the last few minutes before the bell rang. A group of girls "had my number" so to speak, and to my dismay the bully from elementary school was there too. Ugh! I couldn't win.

Over the next two years, I was an outcast. I was never invited to parties, or if I was it was only to find out I had been invited on purpose to be bullied at a slumber party or get together. Invariably, I ended up calling my mother to come get me. I never told my mom about it; I only said I wanted to come home, and she never pressed the issue. On the bright side, through those two years, I managed to put my separateness aside long enough to have a boyfriend. He was oblivious to how I was being treated. On the few occasions when he was witness to it, he would gaze at me and wonder why but never interfere on my behalf. I don't blame him.

Finally, it was off to high school, and the bullying stopped. I liked high school because no one was mean to me anymore, but the separateness remained. I put all my energy into my boyfriend. I thought if I could get all that I needed out of him I wouldn't need friends. Then he moved.

Chapter Five
Worms

During my childhood, something was going on at home. My earliest memories began at the age of two. I had issues involving falling asleep and waking up during the night, not exactly nightmares but they may as well have been.

I don't have any recollection of my parents living or being together other than a brief two weeks when I was nine. In 1968, I lived with my mom and my older brother on the top floor of a renovated old house in Trenton, New Jersey. My parents had moved there from Fort Worth, Texas, to be near some distant family member of my dad's, but the marriage did not last, and he went back to Florida where he was raised and had met my mother.

It was cold all the time. My mom was single and not getting any financial support from anyone, so the lady downstairs watched us during the days while my mother worked. We called her Nanny. She was nice enough and a blessing to my mother so she could go to work as a secretary during the day. However, most nights just when my mom was trying to get us to bed so she could enjoy a few minutes of solitude before retiring herself, I would wake up crying. I wasn't exactly asleep yet, but I would begin to cry and say, "They're on me! They're on me! The worms! They're on me!"

I slept on a twin-sized metal bed in the middle of the floor with little other furniture in the room. My mom would come in and say, "There's nothing on you. It's okay." I would insist, however, and she would proceed to remove my pajamas and show me there were no worms. She would wrap me back in my pajamas, and I would let her leave, but just as soon as I started drifting off to sleep again, I would feel the tingles on my head and legs and arms and start yelling for my mom. She would come back in my room, and this time she would go as far as to remove my pillowcase and sheets to show me there were no worms. Eventually, exhausted, we would both drift off and sleep through the night.

These nighttime issues became progressively worse as I got older, and by the time I was in elementary school, I was terrified to go to sleep at all. I would spend an hour each night begging either my mom and/or my older brother to let me sleep with them. I wasn't exactly sure what I was afraid of or what was happening while I was asleep, but I was terrified. So much so that I would cling to my children's Bible and lie with it in my arms with all the lights on in my room all night long. I would sleep so lightly that it was as if I hadn't slept at all.

As the years went on, I even began staying up all night in the living room with the lights on, crying and clutching my Bible to my breast for nights in a row. I still went to school during the day. I was sure to be quiet on those nights so as not to wake my family and be sent off to my room. Tired and worn out, after about three nights, I could no longer stay awake and would fall into bed exhausted to the point where I just passed out. Then the next night would start another series of sleepless nights.

This went on for years until I got to high school and discovered beer and drugs. These were the answer to all my nighttime problems. I could finally numb myself to who I was and how I existed during the days and nights. The drugs and alcohol would dull the sensitivities I experienced during my interactions with people and their energy. I couldn't believe it! I was relieved and, most of all, the intoxication transformed my ability to fall asleep and stay asleep without incident. I still slept with a night light and have one to this day. The possibility of a nightmare was always lurking, however, so on nights when I wasn't high, the fear would set in, and I would stay up. Little did I know this trend of drowning out my nighttime issues would lead to decades of using substances, including antidepressants, to gain enough courage to sleep and walk through life as I knew it. It wasn't until I got sober and left my third husband in the summer of 2020 that, just like that, the dreams came rushing back.

Chapter Six
Couple at the Bar

Not only were the dreams back, but they returned with the addition of voices talking to me. Night after night, there was something new to see and someone else to hear. It was on like gangbusters! Unlike when I was young, however, I could remember everything with a clarity I had not experienced in my younger years. I could see everything from the fabric on someone's shirt to how they had their hair combed and what their house looked like. I could hear them speak to me and explain situations they were in.

In one of the earliest "dreams," I saw a man and a woman coming out of a bar. Without moving her lips, she said to me, "Do you see him? Do you see how drunk he is? We are going to get in his truck now and drive up the road, and we're both going to die because he's drunk! I don't even want to marry him, but he asked me in front of his whole family! He asked me here with this in mind, but I had no idea that was why he asked me to come!"

I just stood there or rather hovered there looking at her long blonde hair and distraught facial expression. I could see the color of the fabric of her fiancé's shirt: red and blue. It was cold and snowing. They were both wearing coats that were not zipped. I could feel her misery and hopelessness. I could see his intoxication. I didn't know what to do or say. I just watched. Then, I saw a man drive her fiancé's big black truck up to the entrance of the bar, and they both got in. Bang! I was awake.

It was so vivid! Too vivid. I could even tell what decade it was, the 1970s. How was I able to do this? Was this what had been happening all those years ago? If I could communicate with people who had passed, how had I kept it closed off all these years? The bigger question was, why was I there in that couple's experience just prior to dying? Was I supposed to do something? Say something? What was my role exactly? Was it just to listen or merely to observe? I felt it had to be something deeper.

I was terrified again, but this time I knew I was seeing these scenes and hearing these people for a reason. Perhaps these visions were what I was meant to do all along. Perhaps this gift was given to me, but, until I was ready for it, they just appeared to be nightmares.

Decades of not knowing who I was, why I was here, and why I felt like such an outsider were about to be understood over the next several months with the help of my psychic mentor. Through my sessions with her over the next sixteen months, so many things were revealed to me but not just through her. My spirit guides started "talking" to me as I was nodding off at night, during sleep, and in those brief moments before I became awake each morning. It all started to make sense. There was nothing wrong with me. In fact, all was in order. A grand order that I had agreed to before incarnating in this lifetime. All my plans were laid out before my birth. All my previous lifetimes were coming together for this moment, this lifetime. My own grand finale.

Chapter Seven
Indiana

"All of Indiana is written in pain!" I heard. The sound of a camera bulb flashing in a series of three times followed. I saw dead teen boys—a close up of their faces with their dead, cold eyes looking up into space. Flash, flash, flash! I saw a red pickup with several teen boys in the bed of the truck, standing up as he drove across a field. I could not make out the driver, but I knew he was there.

Each one of the boys went by a different nickname. One was "the navigator;" another was "the funny one." They worked the land of the man driving the truck. They were displaced teens who had troubled home lives, so they became runaways. This man took them in and gave them a place to live and food in exchange for working his land. The bad news was he was killing them. One by one he killed them. I saw them dead but didn't know how he was doing it. An older lady, the truck driver's mother, was inside her house with a girl, her daughter. In the kitchen were several boys, but they didn't know their days were numbered.

I could see every detail of the home down to the knitted throw blanket on the back of the couch. The woman was strict and ran the house, but her son, the truck driver, was twisted and murdered the boys. She knew and let him. Like a film camera, I panned to the backyard where the truck driver sat on an overturned, empty 10-gallon paint bucket. As he contemplated what he had done, he looked out in front of him toward an empty pool covered in a clear plastic tarp. He sat with his head leaning on his hand. I knew he was a serial killer. Bang! I was awake.

A few weeks after this, a string of dreams I'd already had about a month earlier replayed in my mind. I asked my guides, "Why am I here again?"

They answered, "Look around."

I was in a back alley. It was Indiana. I saw two young African American men standing with nothing on but their jeans. It was dark outside, and one man was standing over the body of another young African American man who had been shot. The victim was bleeding out. I scanned the scene and noticed a gas station that I had not seen when I was "there" previously. I looked farther down the alleyway and saw a highway overpass. I continued to scout the scenes I was shown. Then I heard a sound like a cell phone when a call drops, and I was awake.

I had a session with my mentor a few days later and asked her about this dream sequence. She told me that my guides wanted me to go back into this set of dreams because they all took place in Indiana, but there was another piece of information I had not located. She asked me to close my eyes and go back in. After I did, she said, "Look around again. What do you see?" I looked beyond the dumpster that was in the alley where the murder of the young African American man took place and saw a carport with the red truck parked underneath.

Chapter Eight
The Yellow House

All of us have vivid dreams at some point in our lives, and I believe they mean something. They may carry a message from our spirit guide(s) or express something our subconscious needs to work out, but in my case I wasn't asleep during these powerful encounters. I was naturally able to hold myself in a lucid state or what is called the theta brainwave state. This can be done in several ways; one familiar way is through hypnotherapy. We reach theta state when our brain activity is much slower than it is during our normal, waking lives. Theta state allows for communication to occur from one side of the veil to the other, where psychics connect and garner divine information for those they read. I later confirmed through research that this was indeed the state which most psychics maintain during readings.

I could wake to the point I was in a theta or *lucid* state, which is just on the edge of sleep but still not in delta brainwaves (sleep state). I could hold myself there in that "between" state, not quite asleep but not fully awake either. I would realize I was no longer in my bed in the traditional sense. My body was there, but energetically I was out of my body and in another location. I could see what was happening and interact with people as well as communicate with my angels or spirit guides. I interacted with my spirit guides by asking questions, which they answered usually with images they would send but sometimes verbally. I kept my eyes closed and carried on with the task at hand.

I was standing in the front yard of a small yellow house. There was no paved driveway, just a path of flattened grass made over time by repeated driving. I stood in front of three brick arches painted the same yellow as the house at the start of the yard. I looked over and there, walking toward me, was a young man about twenty-eight years old. He had beautiful blonde hair combed high off his forehead and wore a tan corduroy jacket with soft cream-colored wool lining the inside. He had a great big smile on his face and appeared to be glad to see me. What was remarkable, however, was he was translucent. He walked toward me, and I could feel his energy pass right through me. He wanted me to follow him to the front door of the yellow house. I walked behind him somewhat hesitantly and noticed he was now holding a three-year-old little girl whom he passed to a woman standing next to him as he reached the front door. The little girl was asleep. I sensed this woman, also in her twenties, was his sister. Standing several feet behind her was another older woman. I felt she was their mother and grandmother to the little girl.

The blonde man opened the door and walked inside with his sister still holding her little girl, and the grandmother followed. I made my way across the yard. When I looked down, I could see my legs and feet as well as my arms and hands as they swung when I walked. They appeared to be surrounded in a gray misty outline, but I was too concerned with getting inside the house to perceive what was going to happen.

I walked inside and was immediately drawn towards a bedroom off to the left. When I went through the frame of the bedroom door, I witnessed an altercation. Three plain clothes detectives stood inside the bedroom, and two of them held the blonde man down as he struggled as if fighting for his life. The third detective was standing in an opening to a closet in the back of the bedroom, observing what was taking place. I realized again that I was in the late 1970s. The clothes the detectives wore looked like they were out of a *Starsky and Hutch* episode, a series that ran on television in the 1970s and 1980s. The show featured two plain clothes detectives that wore bell bottoms and sported hairstyles of those decades.

The three detectives had long sideburns and handlebar mustaches. A badge hung off the shirt pocket of the detective closest to me, and pens stuck out of the top as well. The blonde man was losing the battle for his life. Without even thinking, I reached out and touched the hand of the detective who was taking his life. I said to him, "Stop now. Look what you're doing." His face collapsed and an expression of realization passed over him. Almost as if he had been drawn out of some type of altered state. His body slumped in exhaustion, and he bowed his head. I quickly turned and began walking down the hallway; again I could see my feet and legs with the misty gray outline.

A few feet down the hall, I stopped in the doorway of another bedroom. There was a 10-year-old little boy, still in his blue and red pajamas, and he looked at me and started pointing towards an air conditioner grate in the wall high up towards the ceiling and then at a second larger grate down near the baseboards. He started removing the grate from the one near the floor and pulled out a gun. He then pointed towards the smaller grate and said to me without moving his lips, "There is another gun up there."

I replied, also without moving my lips, "Put the gun back. Don't take them out again; you will only make it worse." I moved down the hallway and sat on the toilet lid in a back bathroom with pink tile that was the style of the decade. In this bathroom the sister and mother were arguing.

The mother was furious, screaming at the daughter, "How could you do this! Look what you have done!"

The argument escalated, and I felt I had completed what I had come there to do, so I found a back door and began running across the front yard trying to find my way out of this "dream." As I rounded the brick arches at the front of the yard, the blonde man appeared again, still with that huge smile. He passed right through me and headed towards the front door as if to start the story all over again. Bang! My eyes flew open.

I sat up in bed and said out loud, "I'm not scared anymore! If this is what I'm supposed to do, I'm ready to do it!"

I lay back down and prayed for restful sleep. At around 7:00 a.m. I began to roll over and stretch and think about getting up for the day, but once again I was hanging in a lucid state. I heard, "You are a physical miracle." Then I saw a message in my mind, typing out in midair that read, "Everyone must heed the miracle that is everyday life."

Weeks before, I had started a dream log and was recording any vision or message I received. I wrote down what I had heard and seen that morning. I wanted to discuss them with my mentor and see if we could make any sense out of what was happening to me.

A couple of weeks later, we had another session, and I quickly began describing the blonde man and all that had occurred in my dream. I asked her if the angels could shed any light on what had happened. She started by telling me that the gray outline I saw on my legs, feet, arms, and hands was what is called an astral suit. It is something our soul can use when leaving our bodies while we're sleeping to visit other areas of the universe or other dimensions. It was basically a travel suit. She went on to say that the blonde man was indeed deceased but that I had changed the lives of the detective, the ten-year-old boy, and the three-year-old girl. I asked her how I changed things for them, and she replied, "Well, by touching the detective, you changed forever the way he lived his life, and never again did he carry out any injustices against others. As for the children, they didn't die, whereas if you had not been there to tell the ten-year-old boy not to take the guns out of hiding…well, that would have been chaos, and both children would have been killed."

I sat there in disbelief. Slowly, I replied, "Wait! What did you say? You mean I went into a timeline and changed the outcome? How is this possible? What do you mean?"

She said, "Yes, that's what you did. When you touch people, it means something."

My mind was racing. *How could this be true?* I thought. I had been fascinated with psychics my entire adult life but had never heard mention of any kind of time traveling. I told my mentor this and she said, "What I'm hearing for you is Earth angel. They are telling me you are an Earth angel and, as for your fascination with the psychic realm, well, birds of a feather flock together."

Chapter Nine
Spirit Guides and Angels

Exactly who are our spirit guides and angels, and what role do they play in our lives? When I first started this journey back in the fall of 2020, I had no idea. I had heard of guardian angels, but, other than just a kind and loving angel that may look after you from time to time, I didn't know much else. As my sessions with my mentor continued, I also had other teachings that were taking place in my daily life.

Each morning, sometimes with an experience at night and sometimes not, I would feel "urges" to do research. I would get on the internet and what would come to be called "my magic finger" would begin clicking and clicking on different subjects to read about and research. I read articles about the afterlife and near-death experiences and about psychics and mediums who could bring deceased people through to their relatives that were still alive and well on planet Earth. However, I felt I needed to know something deeper. As the weeks passed and I was led to certain topics to research, I came across books that explained exactly how spirit guides and angels worked with us, helping to improve our experiences during our lifetimes.

On one such occasion, I felt direct angel or spirit guide intervention. I was riding in a minivan with my ex-husband, and we were in an argument that was quickly escalating. As we drove down a busy street, he decided to pull over in the empty parking lot of a retail strip. It was late at night; the bars had closed, and we were both intoxicated and angry. When he pulled over, I got out of my seat and opened the van's sliding door. He followed and grabbed me, and we began to struggle. He had not put the van in park. It was still in motion. It should have careened forward into one of the closed stores that were just ahead of us, but as we struggled and fought the van quite suddenly started turning in circles.

Over and over again, it gently turned. Suddenly, I caught a view of what was happening as if I were an onlooker. I could clearly see us fighting in the open van doorway and the van making these gentle circles as we exhausted ourselves. The struggle stopped and he jumped back into the driver's seat and put the van in park.

He turned to me and said, "How did that happen? How was the van just turning like that? It stopped on its own. It's like there was someone driving the van in circles while we fought!"

I didn't know how that was possible at the time. Over the years, however, I recall this incident as a miracle. What should have been at the very least a crash into a building followed by police involvement turned out to be a quiet intervention of love and an acknowledgment of our soul contract working itself out.

As I've learned, each of us has a spirit guide or guardian angel—whatever you choose to call them—who remain with us from birth to death. However, for some people, the guides can change or rather be exchanged for a different spirit guide that is better equipped to deal with a new phase of our lives. It is also common for some people to have more than one spirit guide. These guides help us to see opportunities that come our way and to make decisions that are for our highest and best. They act as our intuition. With love in their heart, they have chosen to act as our guide, and we owe them a debt of gratitude for this service. Somehow, we know them. They may be an ancestor, but many times they were someone we knew in a previous life, and they know us well, so they are qualified for this position. It is not important for them to tell us who they are or what their name is; however, being open to their guidance is essential for a life that runs smoother and more in the flow. We can talk to them just as if they are standing in the same room with us. We can discuss what is going right or wrong in our lives and ask for guidance on how to proceed with different forks in the road.

Let me clarify here that calling on archangels is required if we want to receive their assistance since they are not allowed to interfere unless they are asked. We can also ask our guides to show us signs about questions we have. Just give it a try and see what opens up for you.

Chapter Ten
Two Grand Trines

Early in my awakening process, I felt some discontent not knowing who the guides who so generously helped me through my life were. During my next session, my mentor suggested I get in touch with another psychic she had met at a workshop years earlier, who offered a "psychic bootcamp" that might help expand and refine my abilities. No information had been forthcoming up to this point as to who my guides were, so I thought maybe this new psychic could shed some light on the subject.

After hanging up with my mentor, I found her website and read her biography. She had come into her abilities as a teen after a drug overdose. There was something familiar about her story and I was curious. However, before enrolling in her bootcamp, I thought it best to make a reading appointment and meet her first. I scheduled the appointment, which was five weeks out. Oh, boy, this was going to be a long five weeks of waiting. While filling out my information online, I noticed additional services she offered, one of which was an astrology reading. I would need to provide my birthdate, place, and time. I decided I wanted the astrology reading as well and filled in the information.

The day finally came. As we connected via the internet, I tried to squeeze in all that had happened over the last several weeks as quickly as I could. This included information about drowning out who I was with drugs and alcohol starting in high school.

She replied, "It sounds like your story is very similar to mine."

I then asked if she could tell me who my spirits guides were.

She answered, "Your primary spirit guide is Saint Theresa, but you have about five guides. Two of them are ancestors on your mom's side; they are Italian, and there is also a monk here trying to help with your efforts to meditate."

What? Saint Theresa? I thought to myself. I had no words and sat there staring at the screen.

She went on to say, "They are working on opening your right brain."

Huh? I thought as she continued.

While she was talking to me, she was also staring at a second computer screen which held my natal chart for the astrology reading. I had no idea what a natal chart was at the time, but she continued to tell me that I was not from Earth, and even though I had lived lifetimes upon the planet, my primary place of origin was in the stars. She mentioned the Taurus constellation. I was immediately uncomfortable and didn't ask any questions to get clarification.

She then let out a small gasp and said, "Wow! You have two grand trines on your natal chart! I haven't seen this, and I don't ordinarily show my clients my other screen, but I'm going to turn it around so you can see." She proceeded to turn the second monitor towards me, and I could make out a circle with different triangular shapes inside of it, but I didn't know what I was examining. She tried to show me the two trines, and I nodded as if I saw them, but I didn't.

She went on to discuss other topics. She told me that during my travels at night I was going around cleaning up karma. She said I would write a book one day and would talk about what had happened with my last husband. In addition, within three to five years, I would make a trip to Italy and have a direct experience with Saint Theresa of Avila. She explained that I had been a nun in a previous life and Saint Theresa had been with me for a long time. Finally, she recommended an author, Brian Weiss, M.D., who was a pioneer in past life regression therapy and said I should try to find some of his books and ended with the comment, "I don't know why, but they say you have to do this alone."

When the reading was over, I again went to my room, lay down, and tried to absorb all that I heard. The information was coming faster than I could process. Day after day, I would be guided to books. I would get in my car and head to the library and go right to the section about metaphysics, near-death experiences, psychics, mediums, and trance channelers. I would check out the maximum number of books the library would allow, take them home, plow through them, and haul them back to the library, only to check out another stack to take home and devour.

In addition to the books, I would also be guided to watch certain mediums and hypnotherapists and channelers on the internet or the Gaia channel. I was watching and becoming educated on many different types of metaphysical talent, such as Dolores Cannon, Suzanne Giesemann, Allison DuBois, Matias De Stefano, and many more. My magic finger was at work all day. This would carry on for eight to twelve hours a day seven days a week for weeks. I fell exhausted into bed each night and sometimes still had "nightwork" to do. My dream journal was filling, and sessions with my mentor were now regular.

During another session, I told my mentor, "I feel like I'm in some sort of accelerated school. I'm exhausted, but I can't stop."

She replied, "You *are* in an accelerated school. They are telling me that you spent too much time on your soul contract and now they have to get you up to speed."

Up to speed for what? I wondered.

Chapter Eleven
Holy Work

One dream came to me more than once. I started having this dream prior to leaving my husband. I was stomach down on top of a cross that was laying on the ground. My arms were out just like Jesus at the crucifixion, but I was facing the cross, not looking outward. As I lay on the cross in a white gown, I began to panic and say, "I don't know; I don't know! I just don't know if I'm ready for this!" Try as I might, however, my body would begin to slowly raise into the air. As I trembled and looked down from an ever-increasing height, I could see an empty parking lot. The parking lot was lit with one towering flood lamp and was surrounded by a tall wooden fence. What was different about this fence, however, was that a large black hole went through it. I continued floating up above the light, and when I looked over I saw a man dressed all in white coming through the black hole. Everything he wore—shoes, pants, shirt, and jacket—were white. He was running. As he crossed the parking lot, he looked up and saw me. I waved my hand in an indication that he should get behind me, though I'm still up there floating in the air, belly down. Just after he took cover behind me, another man popped through the black hole. He was dressed entirely in black and was pursuing the man in white. I lifted my arm and pointed at the man in black with one finger and said, "No, you don't." Just like that, he was gone.

I opened my eyes and said to my guides, "I've seen this vision several times, but I still don't know what it means."

A few weeks later, I described this recurring dream to my mentor and told her that I would also hear the Christmas carol "Silent Night, Holy Night." She began to explain that the work I did at night was holy work, and my guides were telling me so. They were also showing me a glimpse of a future life where it would be my responsibility to guard this portal and send the bad guys back where they came from.

During the last few minutes of each session I have with my mentor, I ask for a message from my guides. I had been feeling insecure about the psychic abilities I was learning about as well as the glimpses into other lives they were showing me. The following was their response to my questions about my insecurities:

"Go with what you know, work with what has been given, draw conclusions based on what you are receiving in the now. It is not for you to concern yourself with the future at this time. Be in the space of receiving and know that you are much loved and that you are guided on this path to embracing your full purpose. We walk with you every step of the way, we clear the path ahead, we remove the brambles, we remove the rough patches, and we present a clear path forward. It is up to you whether you choose to walk it or to walk alongside where the brambles are. There is much that is awaiting you, there is much that you cannot yet see, and there is a reason for this. Too much information too soon can close your eyes to possibilities when you're not ready. You must learn to crawl before you can walk. In previous lifetimes you have done all of these things and more. In this lifetime you have been focusing more on soul wound healing, and now is the time for the purpose to be at the forefront. Embrace this. Allow us to show you the way. Easy, hard—think not in these terms. Think in terms of flowing. We offer a raft on the river of life. Take the raft and allow us to guide you with the currents of Source. This is our answer."

Chapter Twelve
Kundalini Rising

In the fall of 2020, I was lying in bed while memories of a beautiful male pit bull named Charlie that I used to own with my ex flooded my mind. My sweet pit bull had suffered an early death due to a heart attack at the young age of eight. I began to cry and called out to him, telling him I was sorry for all the arguing that his daddy and I did in front of him and the other dogs that brought them so much stress. If he heard the slightest raised voice between my husband and me or it even vaguely appeared an argument was about to begin, he would start to tremble all over. Thinking about it made me so sad, and my heart was crushed recalling his stress.

Suddenly, I felt an increase in emotion. Almost too much to handle. The crying got louder and more severe. I said to myself, "What is happening here?"

As my emotions escalated, a sensation began at the base of my neck. It was warm and felt like it was glowing. As I continued sobbing and wondering what the sensation was, it began to move down towards the base of my spine. Slowly it traveled, taking that warmth with it until finally it landed in my pelvis, and I felt as if I was going to pee on myself. It stopped as quickly as it started, and the crying ended at the same moment. I pulled the covers back and went to the bathroom to check my clothes.

As I got back in bed and pulled the covers up to my chin, I whispered, "What was that?" Later, I would read about kundalini rising. I was not familiar with this concept at the time, but through my research I learned it is a common occurrence in people who experience a sudden awakening.

Kundalini is a Hindu term referring to the divine feminine energy at the base of the spine in the root chakra or muladhara. Chakras are energy centers that run along the spine starting at the bottom of the coccyx and going all the way to the top of the head. There are other chakras, but the seven that run along the spine are the ones through which kundalini flows. This energy is an expression of the divine feminine, the ethereal essence of the goddess. People say that life changes forever once the kundalini awakens. This energy shifts the being on all levels—physical, mental, emotional, and spiritual, creating an evolution of consciousness. Perhaps the night of the warm glow driving down my spine was an answer to the call I made in my closet that day just a few weeks earlier.

Chapter Thirteen
Slow Motion

My beloved dogs were not the only ones who suffered while my third husband and I acted out our soul contract. My second husband and my children also witnessed things between two adults they should never have had to see or hear.

The father of all my children is a kind soul, and I couldn't have asked for a better match to be their dad. I believe in my heart this arrangement was an agreement we made while creating our own blueprints for this lifetime. I cannot thank him enough for all the kindness and generosity he has shown me through thick and thin.

I remember clearly the first time I saw him. It was as if time slowed to a crawl. I was at a party in college in a crowded house full of students drinking, listening to music, and socializing. I made my way through the packed living room and looked over because I heard someone singing a recently released Red Hot Chili Pepper's song that I particularly enjoyed. As I turned my head, there was a parting of people just wide enough for me to see a blonde-haired young man sitting on some pillows on the floor singing. Students were listening and cheering him on but, as I gazed at him, he felt strangely familiar. It all happened in slow motion.

After a few minutes, I turned to a girlfriend and said quite confidently, "That is my next husband. He is going to be the father of my kids." Somehow, I just knew.

He and I met later that evening, and one thing led to another. Shortly after my divorce from my first husband was finalized, we started planning our own wedding. We graduated on the same day at the same ceremony during the spring of 1993, and a few weeks later we were planning our move to Dallas.

After getting settled in our new apartment in Dallas, we quickly decided we were ready to start a family. Over the course of the next few years, we had a daughter and two sons. After my last son was born in 1998, we had three kids under three years old. I truly thought this was it for me. I believed I had found my true love and would live happily ever after being his wife and raising the kids. Unfortunately, that was not to be the case.

Try as I did to be a good wife (and this was a big effort because I had never seen what a good marriage looked like), I proved to be too overpowering for him and way too demanding for his gentle soul. He had difficulty dealing with my forceful personality, and before we knew it our marriage was struggling. There was more to the story, and each of us had our own contributions to the demise of the marriage. Suffice it to say that by 2005 we were calling it quits, and I moved to an apartment near him and the children. Yes, I thought it would be best if the children stayed with him. I can't explain this decision other than to say I knew there was more to come for me, and the best environment for the kids would be to remain with him as much as possible.

Chapter Fourteen
Moving On

The next several years found me again drowning myself in drugs and alcohol. I was what they call a functioning user. If you had met me at the time, you probably wouldn't have known I had a problem. However, it was there, and I was stumbling through life at that point. One evening, I went by a local bar to see some friends. I walked in and stood talking to my friends but could sense someone looking at me. I shrugged it off and went to the bar to order a drink. Turns out that someone was to become my third husband.

Now, when I say "husband," I mean it in almost every sense of the word. I wore a ring and we referred to each other as husband and wife, but a ceremony never took place. Something deep inside each of us prevented us from taking this step, and we went along for thirteen years never having gotten legally married. We lived together, however, and after a time I began sharing custody with the father of my children, which was how they were exposed to the storm that was our relationship.

Now, the children are grown and are released from that toxicity since I am no longer with my third husband. I am so relieved for them. My oldest son moved near the northwestern part of the country, got married, and has a daughter. My oldest child (my daughter) and my youngest (my other son) still live with their dad and are each pursuing different journeys into adulthood. Therapy is a part of their lives as they try to repair the wounds of the past. I wholeheartedly love and support their healing. My prayer is that each of them can heal fully and go on to lead healthy, happy lives.

One clarification: While married to the father of my children and during my subsequent pregnancies, I did not partake in any drugs or alcohol (other than an occasional glass of wine during dinner). I did, however, take prescription antidepressants from time to time. You see, I was trying to keep my abilities at bay; I just didn't know it. I truly believed there was something wrong with me, and the nighttime hours were still a struggle. In addition, I frequently felt dizzy sensations between my eyes and lightheadedness I couldn't explain. Naturally, I thought I must be going a little crazy because I didn't feel *right* in my head. I wasn't getting nightmares or dreams so often anymore, but the thought of going to sleep was always difficult at best. I struggled to feel normal, and underneath there was always something nagging at me.

Chapter Fifteen
Saint Hildegard of Vinzgau

Winter of 2020 found me sitting on my couch one evening watching television, and I suddenly started humming "Sau Gan," a Welsh lullaby written by an anonymous composer. It was first recorded in print around 1800, and the lyrics were captured by the Welsh folklorist Robert Bryan (1858–1920). The song's title simply means lullaby (*suo* = lull; *cân* = song). I was familiar with the lullaby from one of my favorite movies *Empire of the Sun*, directed by Stephen Spielberg; however, it had been well over a decade since I had seen the movie.

The lyrics to Sau Gan are translated as follows:

Sleep, my baby, at my breast,
Tis a mother's arms around you.
Make yourself a snug, warm nest.
Feel my love forever new.
Harm will not meet you in sleep,
Hurt will always pass you by.
Child beloved, always you'll keep,
In sleep gentle, on your mother's breast
Do not fear the sound, it's a breeze
Brushing leaves against the door.
Do not dread the murmuring seas,
Lonely waves washing the shore.
Sleep, child mine, there's nothing here
While in slumber at my breast.
Angels smiling, have no fear.
Holy angels guard your rest.

(Received 7/19/2021)

While I was about to fall asleep that night, I heard the words, "Saint Hildegard in the time of Charlemagne."

During the next session with my mentor, I inquired about this message that came through in the song and the messenger who had sent it to me. My mentor explained it was a direct message from Spirit to ease my worries about falling asleep at night. Saint Hildegard of Vinzgau had sent the message and was my mother in a previous lifetime, where I had not lived long and died in my late teens. Saint Hildegard of Vinzgau, a queen consort of Frankish descent, was Charlemagne's second wife. She was also the mother of the Louis the Pious.

My mentor commented, "Well! She was persistent, wasn't she?"

I was honored to know of this previous life with Saint Hildegard of Vinzgau and felt her kindness and maternal love in a visceral way that is difficult for me to convey. Let's just say I felt coddled and protected by her presence. I honor her existence in my life then and now.

Chapter Sixteen
Sickle Dream

January 2021 had arrived, and I had a dream that I was with someone, and we were looking at an ad in the paper for a missing woman. The missing woman's five-year old son appeared and asked, "Do you know where my mother is?" I knew my ex-husband had been dating this woman, so I asked the child for the mother's phone number. I had a horrible feeling that something had happened to her.

I told the boy, "I'll call her but I'm sure he is looking at her phone and will know that I am calling." I called anyway, and, sure enough, he answered her phone and lied about where she was. I pretended to be a friend of hers, but he knew it was me. I saw myself inside his house, and I was making my way towards the door. I felt he was going to confront me. I took my time getting to the door because I wanted the confrontation. In my dream, I'm seeing myself doing these things, but it's not really me; it's the woman.

The woman attacked him with a pair of scissors, knowing he would be able to overtake her. I continued to see my face on her body. He counter attacked with what looked like a sickle blade but ran the blade under her feet as she lunged towards him. As she fell, he gave up and dropped the sickle.

She began yelling, "What were you going to do? Were you going to kill me while your parole officer is waiting outside?"

She was provoking him on his way outside to be arrested. I then saw his probation officer standing in the front yard with his arms folded against his chest. Standing next to him was a lady with shoulder length blonde hair dressed in a white gown.

After consulting my mentor, I learned that this was a vision my guides had shown me. They were showing me that my ex-husband was in a relationship with this woman that was more toxic than ours had been. The "person" who was looking at the ad with me in the vision turned out to be my own guide. The boy was a baby my ex-husband's girlfriend lost shortly after birth due to sudden infant death syndrome five years prior. My mentor further explained that, although the son had died as an infant, he continued "growing up" on the other side of the veil and was contacting me because he was worried about his mom and wanted me to help locate her. My mentor said I was seeing my face on the woman's body because I did not know what she looked like. I had never met the girlfriend. My mentor went on to explain that the blonde woman in the white robe standing next to the probation officer was his spirit guide. The probation officer was there because my ex-husband was going back to jail at some point for violation of probation. My mentor commented, "Add seeing people's spirit guides to your list of gifts."

A month later, during a rare visit from my ex-husband, he began describing a fight he recently had with his new girlfriend. I incredulously listened to him prattle on. I could not believe he was so heartless as to treat me as if I were some buddy of his with whom he could discuss his new relationship as if it didn't hurt me. He had not changed one bit in his callousness. I was simultaneously hurt and angry.

He described how she had attacked him with a pair of scissors and went on about how mentally unstable she was. I replied, "I know this already and her son is quite worried about her."

He turned and looked at me and asked, "How do you know about her son? He died several years ago. And the scissors? How did you know she attacked me with scissors?"

I replied, "I can see things. Don't you remember all the psychic shows I used to watch? Well, I can do that too."

I sent him on his way, and he did not make another visit for several weeks.

When he showed up again, he called from the parking lot of my apartment complex. I said I would come outside because I didn't want him in my apartment anymore. I was still hurt, and it was best for me to keep him at bay.

I walked outside and he got out of his truck. I asked him why he was there, and he proceeded to tell me, yet again, of another fight with his girlfriend. I reluctantly listened and sarcastically replied, "Why don't you break up with her if it's so miserable?"

He looked at me and said, "Sometimes, when we fight, I just want to strangle the life out of her."

I was staring at him while he said this and suddenly his eyes changed to black. It was as quick as a flash, but I was sure I had seen it. I stepped back a few feet and said I had somewhere to be, quickly turned, and headed back to my apartment.

That was it for me. I knew his dark side had taken over and he was no longer stable. I began to avoid his occasional calls and eventually changed my phone number.

Chapter Seventeen
Teacher

I want to briefly discuss how I have always known I would be a teacher. Although I won't fulfill this role in the traditional sense, I strongly sense that I will teach in some capacity I am not yet aware of.

When I was in the second grade, a couple of neighborhood girls would come over to play during the summer. We acted out the same scene every time with me wanting to play the role of teacher and them being the students. I was quite selfish with my demand about being the teacher, and they were sweet to accommodate me. Naturally, when I got to college, I knew education was going to be my major.

I met my first husband at the age of fifteen when I was home alone during the summer. I was in my room reading a book when I heard a knock at the front door and went to answer. Standing there was a friend of my older brother. He grinned and asked if my brother was home. I said he wasn't but I would tell my brother he had come by.

He leaned down and said in my face, "Aren't you cute?! I knew he had a sister, but I didn't know it was you."

Again, I experienced that funny feeling that I'd met this person before, and off we went to become boyfriend and girlfriend and eventually husband and wife.

I married him when I was twenty years old. Just weeks after we said, "I do," he received a letter in the mail saying that Texas A&M University had accepted him into their engineering program. I was so excited! This was perfect timing.

We had settled into a small rental house in West University Place, a small city inside the city of Houston, and we had decent enough jobs. However, we were both stagnating in our positions, which held little interest and offered limited opportunity to advance without degrees. We decided he should accept the offer, and a couple of months later we were packed and ready to move to College Station. We had one car and a small U-Haul attached to the back with our meager belongings. We soon settled in, and I got a job with the university while he started classes.

    A year into our experience, I was itching to go to college myself and heard of a junior college branch that was located just across the street from the university. It turned out that I could transfer into the university and start my own journey to receive a degree in education with forty-four hours at the junior college. I enrolled and four years later had a Bachelor of Science degree.

    The marriage did not last, however, and by my senior year we had split. He moved away leaving me to finish my degree alone. Although I had the desire to teach since childhood, as soon as I graduated, I knew teaching children was not for me, so I worked various jobs over my adult life and raised my kids but never taught professionally. However, I still feel the desire to teach in some capacity nagging at me. I would even say to people who asked why I wasn't teaching, "I don't know. It just feels like I should be teaching adults, not children." We then changed the subject and life moved on.

Chapter Eighteen
Starseed

Coming back to my natal chart and its two grand trines, I researched for anything I could find with limited success. Finally giving up, I made an appointment with my mentor to try and get to the bottom of it. As the call started, I described to her what had taken place with the psychic who informed me about the trines. I explained to my mentor that grand trines appeared to be "gifts from God." I went on to tell her about the psychic's expression of surprise that I appeared to have two.

My mentor asked if the other psychic had explained what the gifts were, and I answered, "No." She said she would tune in and see if she could get an answer.

A few minutes later, she opened her eyes and said, "Yes, these are gifts from God, and you have two of them. The first one is the ability at some point to be able to touch people and see their life path, and the second one is a Source energy that has not been on the planet before, but that Source will channel through your hands. You will be giving people a deep, deep level healing." She went on to say that her hands were on fire just talking about it. She explained, "This won't be happening for some time, however, because you need to learn how to hold a great deal of energy so your circuits don't fry."

She then held her hands up to the camera and they looked red and hot.

Here I was speechless again. Slowly, tears started rolling down my face, and a tiny gasp came up from my throat. How could this be? Honestly, I'm just a 5'2", 54-year-old woman from Fort Worth, Texas. Weren't things like that supposed to happen to priests, nuns, monks, or some other type of religious or spiritual person? Those kinds of people seemed so much more deserving of such gifts than me.

After what felt like an hour but was only a few minutes, I started to compose myself and went on to tell her about the other psychic's comments concerning me "being from the stars."

My mentor replied, "I've tried to talk to you about this before. You are a starseed. If you don't want to talk about it, we don't have to. Let me know."

The tears started coming even harder, and I visibly shrank down in my chair but conjured enough courage to say, "No, please go on."

She then asked me about all the research I was doing and if any of the books I was guided to read or documentaries, videos, or series I had seen had me resonating with any particular set of ETs. I glanced over at the table in my living room and sitting on top was a book about Pleiadians. I looked back at her and said quite timidly, "Yes."

"Well..." she said.

To people like my mentor, meaning those who are already familiar with the metaphysical world, this news probably didn't seem so extraordinary, but to me it was just that. I listened to her explain the Pleiadians' significance to the planet and how for thousands of years they (along with many other star races) have been involved in the evolution of humanity. I sat and absorbed all she was telling me. I hung up from the call and sat there a little longer. Slowly, I got up and walked once again to my room. I lay there looking at the ceiling and realized there was oh so much left in this last journey on Earth for me. I had only just begun to tap into what the rest of my life would look like.

The following morning as I began to wake, I heard, "You are a 5D light being. You are from the fifth dimension." I was finally starting to get some answers directly from my guides.

Several months later, I received my own vision and, thus, my own validation of my ultimate purpose for this lifetime. Lying on my couch one afternoon shortly after arriving in my new home, I started getting a vision of deep space. I was not asleep and had just closed my eyes when this vision appeared. What I was seeing was darker and deeper than any telescope could capture or any movie could try to portray. It was a solitary space with only a few tiny new stars twinkling ever so faintly. The space was still but moving slightly in a perpetual motion, and the silence was deafening. Just as suddenly, I saw my own hands, palms facing in and slowly progressing towards me. I sat quietly for a moment pondering what I had just seen and felt gratitude for this communication. This vision portrayed my end goal for this lifetime. How it will unfold remains to be seen.

Chapter Nineteen
Neighborhood Watchman

"Don't hurt me! I'm just a girl."

I was time traveling again. This time I went back 14 years to 2006. I no longer needed my astral suit and often went inside people's bodies energetically as I interacted with them in other dimensions. I was inside a young woman on this occasion. We were frantically looking through a plastic storage unit behind a home that did not belong to her. I could hear her saying inside her head, "I will show him. I'll show him that I can steal things too. I'm just going to find something small I can take to prove to him that I can do it."

As she said these words, she accidentally knocked an empty Folgers can out of the storage unit, and it landed with a bang on the concrete driveway and started rolling. I see everything. The houses were modest, and, instead of a garage, they had a roof extension to park the cars underneath. The driveway where we stood held the plastic storage unit piled high with garage items. Now, she was in a panic. Scared she has been heard, she started to run across the driveway and off into the grass, but it wasn't grass; it was weeds so tall they reached her knees.

I said, "Don't run! Let's get back to the car and get out of here!"

As she turned toward the car, I could see that it was brand new. It was one of those Chevrolets that looked like a car and a truck all in one. The car was cream colored with a matching leather interior. The keys were in the ignition. They still had the paper chain from the dealership.

We tried backing the car up but it was too dark to make out the surroundings. We managed to turn the car around and attempted to drive straight out only to be blocked by a big body muscle car that was backing straight into us! Suddenly, she was in the seat with her head leaning back on the headrest. Still inside her body, I managed to get the window down and could see two Great Danes running back and forth outside the car window, agitated and barking. A tall, thin man with messy black hair and a beard stood right beside the window. He wore a blue and black flannel shirt and held a rifle. The butt of the rifle rested in the crook of his arm.

Slowly rolling my head to the side so I could see him better, I said, "Don't hurt me! I'm just a girl."

This seemed to rouse him out of some sort of trance, and immediately his face changed to an expression of shock. He took off running up the dirt alleyway and went into a backyard that had a chain-link fence and also a wooden one that was built around its inside perimeter and was very high to prevent anyone from seeing inside the yard. However, I was able to watch him go in the back door of the house. The homeowner was an extremely overweight man who played the role of the neighborhood watchman. But he was not the one doing the surveillance because he never left the house. The man with the rifle carried out the neighborhood watch. Bang! I was awake.

A couple of weeks later, I would learn from my mentor that this was the first time the man in the blue flannel shirt had shot a person. Though he had hunted and killed animals, he had never shot a person. Now, he had shot the young woman in the gut. Since my words were able to draw the man out of his daze, he called for help, and she lived. Whew! That was close! I thought, however, how sad it was both for him and the victim that he had shot a human being.

Chapter Twenty
Angel Intervention

Early in my awakening, during the fall of 2020, I was headed out to my local nail shop to get a manicure. Worn out from all the dreams, visions, books, and videos, I just needed a break to do something for myself that was relaxing and felt good. I needed to feel "normal" for a little while, so I got in my car and drove toward the shop.

I lived in a small town on the Gulf Coast of Texas. I had moved there from Houston with my ex-husband in the spring of 2017. He had family there and we wanted to downsize the city we were living in and try to turn our lives around. That was not to be the case with him, but for me it had finally happened.

When I arrived at the shop, I expected to hear the pleasant chatter of the other customers talking to their nail technicians along with the hum of the TV that was mounted on the wall. Instead, I heard a woman in a pedicure chair moaning loudly. I scanned the shop and tried to get a feel for what was happening. Instantly, I sensed a chaotic energy in the room to the point I could feel static electricity on my skin. As I watched the woman and the owner, who was giving her a pedicure, I could not believe my eyes.

The woman was writhing in the chair and moaning as if she were having an orgasm. The discomfort of the customers and the other nail technicians was palpable. I made my way over to the owner who was bent over the moaning woman's feet, trying desperately to stay calm, and asked her, "What is going on?"

She looked up at me hopelessly. Another nail technician waved me over to a different station, and I sat down as my head began to pound. The woman moaned louder and was moving in her chair so violently that the owner could not even tend to her feet. I thought to myself, *Well, if I'm supposed to be able to call on the angels for help, this is as good a time as any.* I bowed my head and opened my crown chakra. I envisioned a column of white light from the heavens coming through my head and all the way down my spine and disappearing into the floor. I silently said, "Angels, I need you! We need help here! I don't exactly know what is wrong with this woman; I suspect drugs, but either way the shop needs you! Please come to our aid and calm this woman, and let's send her home where she can rest."

I opened my eyes and within two minutes the shop fell silent. Everyone started looking around. I glanced over at the woman who had been moaning, and she was asleep! One customer said, "I don't know what just happened, but thank God!"

Had the angels actually shown up? Did I accomplish what I set out to do? Wow! It worked!

A few minutes later, the owner woke the woman because it was time to move her to the waxing room to wax her eyebrows. *Oh no!* I thought. *Is she going to start up again?* However, she moved slowly to the waxing room, and about ten minutes later she emerged with tears streaming down her face saying, "Praise Jesus! I love Jesus! I need to go home and praise Jesus; he is my savior!" She paid for her services and left the shop.

We all started buzzing about what just happened. I said to the customers that remained in the shop, the owner, and other technicians, "I prayed."

One customer turned to me and said, "I don't know what you did, but thank you!"

The rest of my visit was uneventful, and I drove home feeling satisfied and in awe of the angels.

Several weeks later, I went back to the shop, and the owner walked up to me as soon as I arrived and said, "I don't know what you did, but now every time that woman comes in, she sleeps!"

She thanked me several times and went on to explain the woman was a cocaine addict. If the moaning woman could not get cocaine, she would inhale baby powder instead.

Oh, what a horrible existence! I thought. I sent a loving vibe and wish to the woman, praying that she would turn her life around with the help of the angels.

Chapter Twenty-One
Source Conduit

I had just finished eating a quiet breakfast at the local diner. After paying for my breakfast, I walked outside, glanced over, and saw a door to what in the past had been empty office space but now had lettering with the name and contact information for a therapist. I stopped and pulled out my phone to take a picture of it. I had been eating at the diner on and off for four years, and the office space was always empty, but there she was open for business. I was severely depressed because I had just left my husband. I walked around most of the time in a daze. I needed to speak to someone and dig my way out of my depression.

Over the next two days, I kept pulling up the picture of the door on my cell phone and finally called. A recorder came on saying she was in session and would return my call. I left my name and number and hung up. The next day my phone rang, and it was the therapist. She explained that she had just opened her practice at that location and would be happy to see me in a few days. I agreed and we scheduled my first appointment.

My first several meetings with her were all about my ex-husband, and she suggested ways in which I could start the healing process. From the start, it felt naturally easy to talk with her. It was like talking to someone I already knew. As the weeks turned into months, she heard it all. All the dreams and descriptions of what I was seeing and hearing, and not once did she make me feel like I was crazy or had entered a delusional state. Let me tell you, she heard some incredible stories over those months!

On one such occasion, I told her about the "Hoovering for Christ" dream. I had taken to the habit of naming my dreams. With just a simple title, I could experience total recall of what occurred in them. I began to tell her about sending the man in black back through the portal and how my psychic mentor had explained my job of guarding the portal. When I finished describing the dream, she gazed kindly at me and I added, "You know, over the several times I've had this dream, I would feel fear, but how I am able to come to terms with it is to imagine that the man in white is one of my children, and I would do anything to keep them safe."

She nodded and continued gazing at me. Suddenly, words started spilling out of my mouth, "But they are all my children," I blurted.

We both heard it. I jerked my head, and my therapist looked a little startled. What had just happened? Why did I say that? Where had that come from? There were butterflies in my stomach. I nervously sat up, leaned forward to hand her my debit card to pay for my session, and made an appointment for the following week. Then I sheepishly walked out of the office.

Between visits, I had another session with my mentor. Right away I told her about what happened during my last therapy appointment. She closed her eyes and when she opened them again, she said, "That's because you are a Source conduit. Source spoke through you."

Gulp! *Huh? What is a Source conduit?* Once again, tears slowly started making their way down my cheeks. She went on to explain that some people are born with the ability to channel Source (God); in metaphysical circles, it was called being a "Source conduit."

I was not the only person on the planet who had this gift, but I was one of them. I then asked my mentor, "Who is my therapist? Who exactly is she to me?"

She replied, "They are telling me she was your mother in a previous life. You died young in that lifetime at around age eight or nine. This is her lifetime to see you reach your full potential."

Okay, mind blown! Remember, I had never heard of the things I was now learning on a daily basis. My life up to this point was different but not extraordinary. Now, in one short afternoon, I learned I was a Source conduit, and my therapist was my mom in a previous life.

When the call concluded, I went over to the couch, and my precious Larry looked up at me with an expression that said, "I was wondering when you were going to 'get it,' Mom." On some level, Larry recognized who I was more than I did, and I knew in my heart he was here on this planet for me. Thanks for being there for me, Larry. I love you too.

Chapter Twenty-Two
Gatekeeper

"Last night I heard from Archangel Michael," I said to my mentor as we looked at one another through our computer screens. As an angelic channeler herself, my mentor was not too surprised by my statement.

A few weeks before this session, I had come across an ad for crystals on my social media page. *Why was this coming up?* I wondered. Over the years I had been drawn to rocks but not necessarily crystals. This ad, however, was leaping off the page. I quickly searched for the nearest crystal shop and found one on The Strand in Galveston. I jumped in the car and headed down the road towards the ocean.

The Strand is a strip of converted 1800s buildings one block from the Gulf of Mexico that are now loft apartments, souvenir stores, and restaurants. Tourists stroll up and down The Strand shopping, eating, and visiting with one another. The crystal store was at the bottom of one of the converted buildings at the end of the strip. As I walked in, I immediately felt emotional and a little overwhelmed. I scanned the room and saw lots of crystals, but what drew my eye was a table to my right. A trilogy of books about angel experiences sat on top of the table. I immediately felt drawn to one with a green cover, the second book of the trilogy. When I walked up to the counter, a woman introduced herself as the owner of the shop as well as the author of the books. She wore crystals around her neck as well as rings and bracelets. She saw the book I slid onto the counter and said, "I think you will like this one."

I took the book home and devoured it in just over a day. I got back in the car a few days later, arrived back at the store, and bought book three. Once I plowed through book three, I returned once again and bought book one. A few weeks after finishing the trilogy, I visited the store again.

I had found the owner's website shortly after my first visit and noticed she did readings. I made an appointment for a few weeks later, and the time for the reading finally arrived. I reminded her that I was the one who bought all three of her books but had read them in reverse order. She laughed and said, "You read them in the order you were meant to."

The reading was different from my mentor's sessions but helpful, and I enjoyed my time with her. Towards the end of the reading, she said to me, "The angels say you've caught on quickly, and Archangel Michael says for you to ask him to be your gatekeeper." I stared at her for a minute but nodded my head, and we said our goodbyes.

I got into my car and started the engine but sat there for a moment. *How would I go about asking Archangel Michael to be my gatekeeper? What is a gatekeeper?* I decided not to make it complicated. That night while lying in bed desperately trying to relax enough to get some sleep, I started talking to Archangel Michael.

"I heard your request today," I began. "I don't know exactly what a gatekeeper is, but I am honoring your request and asking you if you will be my gatekeeper."

With that, I drifted off to sleep, not knowing what the night would bring. Around 2:00 a.m. I started receiving a message that was being spelled out. It said, "Hello, Melina. My name is Gino." Then it erased the "o" and replaced it with an "a," then removed again and spelled out the entire name, "Giovanni."

"Okay, who is this?" I questioned as I remained in the lucid state. I wasn't getting an answer, so I drifted back off to sleep only to awaken again about 3:30 a.m. to the name "Archangel Michael." It was spelled out three times. After I read the name, the words "royal blue" flashed in front of me. I opened my eyes and had a sudden urge to look on the internet using my cell phone, which was lying next to me on the bed. I searched for images of Archangel Michael. I typed in the words "royal blue" and "Archangel Michael," and right away a beautiful painting popped up on my screen glowing with the color royal blue and Archangel Michael right in the center. Awesome! I put the phone on my pillow, left the picture up, and went back to sleep.

Over the next few weeks, I kept seeing the name Giovanni and finally decided to bring it up to my mentor. After inquiring about him, she said, "He is here to help you with deceased loved ones in spirit. He will be the one bringing spirits forward to you. They will have to go through him first, and he will present them to you."

"Uh, okay." I muttered, once again perplexed but trying not to question too much and just take it in.

I went on to explain about my reading with the crystal store owner and her telling me of Archangel Michael's request. My mentor replied that he would be the one to look out for me during my travels into other dimensions at night. That is what he meant by "gatekeeper." I felt better knowing what a gatekeeper was. After discussing a few other things, we ended the call.

That night as I got ready for bed, I was filled with the usual trepidation over what was in store. My head had barely hit the pillow when I saw a man with shoulder length graying hair that had several black strands still holding on. He looked in a mirror and said, "It took me seven years to get my hair like this."

Just as quickly as he appeared, he was gone. Immediately following the man, a girl who appeared to be from India came into view. She had long, silken black hair that went down to the top of her waist. She wore a beautiful purple outfit trimmed in gold that reminded me of Princess Jasmine from the movie *Aladdin*. She was holding a dance pose with her hands raised gracefully above her head. She said, "Don't I dance beautifully?"

The next night the dead started coming again as soon as I lay my head down and closed my eyes. The visions started with an ensemble of 1970s and '80s TV show music. First, I heard the theme song from *Cagney and Lacey*, then *All in the*

Family, and finally *Columbo*. As strange as this was, I felt it was leading somewhere.

I saw a woman possibly 60 years old with gray hair cut in a bob who was wearing a white T-shirt with a green sweater over it. She held her hands in front of her face and said, "Stop! Don't look at me! Don't look at me!" She was gone pretty quickly.

The next visitor was a little girl roughly four years old. She wore pink pants and a red turtleneck. Her blonde hair was pulled back in a ponytail. She said, "I like my school." I saw her standing in a playground next to one of those climbing bars that were in a hexagon shape. The little girl asked if I could see her mother. For some reason I was filled with an icky feeling but turned and looked over at the mother who was standing nearby. Wearing a long, black fur coat and black sunglasses, she stood just staring back at me with no smile or acknowledgment. Their clothes were from the late 1970s to early 1980s, and the mother's hair was teased and sprayed in the style of the period. I tried to get an idea of why I was feeling this sinking in my stomach, but it was too early in my awakening to discern.

The visions continued with the appearance of another man with thick blonde hair and a heavy blonde mustache. Instead of speaking, he used symbols to communicate. I was shown a black motorcycle, a desert road, a cactus, and a blue mailbox like the ones at the post office. Next, I received a vision of a female cop standing in a kitchen that served the needy. I wasn't sure what to make of her appearance in this sequence since she neither spoke nor presented symbols.

I finished the night with a dream of being in a house I did not recognize as a robot-looking person without a face stood next to me trying to tell me how he had died. I told him, "I'm really not quite ready yet."

I walked out of the room to a landing on the other side of a staircase, and he followed. He kept running his finger across his neck and saying, "My throat was cut all the way to my epiglottis." I could barely bring myself to look at him and did not understand why he appeared as a robot. He looked like he came straight out of *I, Robot*, just with no face. That's the last dream I remember that night. Finally, I was able to get some sleep.

Chapter Twenty-Three
You Are Not Girl

I had finally fallen asleep after two hours of tossing and turning. I was having a hard time turning off my brain from analyzing all that was happening to me. I felt overwhelmed and my life had become quite surreal. As I began to drift off to sleep, the dream started.

I was naked sitting on a throne. My breasts were blurred out so they were not visible. The throne was white and not ornate. God was standing right in front of me. I looked microscopic next to him and could only see the bottom of his white robe. He said to me in a booming voice, "You are not girl, but you are girl!"

I looked up timidly but said nothing. Suddenly, I saw a red valentine-shaped heart over my pelvis. I looked down at it and looked back up towards God. There was a flash and I saw a five of spades card with a seven of hearts on top and slightly to the side of it. My eyes shot open, and my heart was beating loudly in my chest. What had I just seen? What did it mean? How could I be a girl and not a girl?

Later, during a session with my mentor, she explained that I had a visit from Source and that he was telling me that my life was no longer about relationships, sex, or gender. My life had taken on a new purpose and needed my focus. When I asked her why I was sitting on a throne, she replied, "That is because you are psychic royalty." She further explained that the seven of hearts was the card of the divine.

I didn't really know what to make of her statement because I sure didn't feel like psychic royalty.

Chapter Twenty-Four
Mob Boss's Wife

I was standing in a gorgeous satin wedding gown. My hair elegantly twisted high on my head. I could see my long sinewy fingers. I stared out an open window in a small room in the back of an ornate Catholic church. The window screen was broken, and it billowed in the wind. I was smoking a cigarette and just daydreaming. Considering it was my wedding day, I was not at all excited. I said to myself, "What is taking so long for them to check the families for weapons? Can't we get on with this wedding already?"

Looking through the door I had cracked just enough to peer out at the attendees, I could make out some of the male guests being frisked and saw they were wearing spats, the linen coverings that buttoned along the side and covered the top of their shoes, a fashion accessory of the 1920s. I figured it was 1925. I closed the door and continued smoking my cigarette, blowing the smoke out the window. Just then the door opened and my older brother from my current lifetime walked in. It was not his face, but I recognized his soul.

He asked, "Why are you smoking? Are you high?"

I replied, "No, I'm not high and I'm fine, so let's just do this."

I threw my cigarette out the window, took his arm, and headed out to the ceremony. Then, I woke up.

"What in the world was that?" I asked myself.

During my next session with my mentor, I asked about this dream. She told me it was not a dream at all and said, "This was a previous lifetime of yours. The reason you were so nonchalant about your wedding day was that you had agreed to marry a mob boss, and you overlooked his girlfriends and sketchy means of making money because he could offer you the life you wanted." She added, "It was

1925 and, yes, the brother you have now was also your brother then."

Okay…

That was the beginning of my ability to recall my past lifetimes and parallel lives. Over the next few weeks, more visions of these lives arose in my consciousness. What I was doing was getting into my own Akashic Records—another indication that my abilities were growing.

Chapter Twenty-Five
We Are the Pleiadians

I was in a skyscraper working an office job with several coworkers on the same floor. As I sat at my desk, I noticed most of my coworkers gathering at the window, where a strange giant cloud formation was swirling in the sky. In disbelief, they pointed and gasped as the cloud began to *open*. I walked up behind the crowd at the window and looked up at the swirling cloud. Immediately, I said to myself, "Oh, boy; they're here for me."

Crouching down, I slinked back to my desk. I was hoping the beings I knew were inside the craft just on the other side of the cloud would think I was not there. Well, no such luck. Suddenly, an elevator appeared right next to my desk where there was none before. I quickly crawled under the desk. *Oh! They're going to know I'm hiding here. It's too obvious!* I thought. So, I quickly scurried on my hands and knees and tried to conceal myself behind my chair.

Well, that was futile because they knew exactly where I was. As I peered around the chair, I saw the elevator door open, and a pulsing red light emanated from it. I could discern the feet of an ET start to step off the elevator, turning towards my desk. The chair was swooshed to the side without anyone even touching it, and there I was totally exposed! I could feel the fear inside my throat, but just then I saw the arms of my ex-husband unfold, and I heard his voice say, "Don't be scared. It's time to come out."

Oh, they are quite clever! I thought. Knowing once in the beginning of our relationship, my last husband had been my security blanket, they were certain I would automatically relax. *Nice!* The imposter even wore one of his favorite shirts so I could be sure it was him. It was funny though; they didn't get his arms quite right. He was muscular and these arms were somewhat thin. No matter. I was at ease, and I woke up.

As I lay on my pillow trying to rationalize what I had just seen in my dream, I was filled with a knowing that all was going to be okay. The sooner I opened myself to their guidance, the sooner I would align with who I really was. All was well and it felt perfect.

On another such occasion in a dream, a written message came with a visit from my star family. After returning from a vacation with my daughter in Kauai, I went to bed and fell asleep rather easily that night. A couple of hours later, however, the dream started.

I saw a friend of mine flying in a plane overhead. I could see her face clearly through the small window though she was in the sky. I asked her telepathically, "What is going on? Why are they here?"

She answered, "They are here to take those who are ready to go."

I looked over and saw the largest spaceship I could have possibly imagined. It was gigantic! Instead of landing like in the movies, the spacecraft stopped and turned itself vertically so I could see its bottom, which looked like a maze with cutouts and turns. I stared in disbelief at the sheer size of the vessel. The people on the ground beside me who stood closer to the ship looked like tiny ants. As I gazed again at the bottom of the ship, words started to type themselves out: "We are the Pleiadians. We are here to help humanity. We have always been with you. We are here for the greater good."

I read the message and then telepathically asked, "Can I go too?"

I heard an immediate answer, "No, you are not done yet."

I was sad, but I couldn't let myself get emotional or I would not be able to have any contentment while I remained on Earth, so I sucked it up and said to myself, "Okay, I can do this." Then I woke up.

A few days later, I spoke with my mentor, and she assured me what I was seeing was the real deal. My spirit guides were communicating with me during lucid sleep, and they were showing me things for my information and learning. I asked her again if she could tell me anything about my spirit guides. This was when I knew they had decided to share a little more.

She closed her eyes and replied, "Your guides are a collective from your home star system. There are several of them, and they speak to you as a collective or sometimes one on one."

I didn't ask but assumed Saint Theresa was still among my guides, or perhaps her role had ended and now I was being guided by a collective from where I originated, or possibly they had always been with me. I do not know for sure about the exact makeup of my group of guides, and I'm content not knowing for now.

Chapter Twenty-Six
The Plunger

I saw a dead woman—a close-up of her face with her eyes staring up and devoid of life. She was lying on the living room floor beaten to death. A man, her ex-husband, stood over her, enraged. He had reddish blonde hair with a moustache. Then, I was shown two women. One was his girlfriend and the other his ex-wife, the dead woman on the floor. He was still in love with his ex-wife.

Suddenly, I was sitting in the living room with the ex-wife prior to her death. I was desperately trying to convince her that her estranged husband was on his way to kill her.

She laughed and said, "Well, at least I have control over my dreams! I would never dream anything like that just days before my daughter's birthday party!"

I explained to her that despite having a girlfriend her ex-husband had never gotten over their divorce and resented her for being able to move on so smoothly.

I said urgently, "You should be glad I can do this! If I couldn't, there wouldn't be any birthday party for your daughter!"

She continued to brush me off. However, I could sense him nearby and decided to head for the front door.

I was outside now at night. A huge flood light lit her entire front yard. I could see the exterior of the house, the property, and the neighborhood. The house was Tudor style, and I realized I was in the early 1990s. An elongated, narrow open window overlooked the front yard from the kitchen. Inside the window, a tiny dog sat on a window seat, yapping loudly at me. He jumped out of the window and made a beeline for me. I scooped him up and said, "Be quiet! Something's off."

The ex-wife was now outside with me. She said, "See, he can't do anything to me. I've had this flood light installed."

I could sense her husband lurking in the yard.

The neighborhood was upper middle class, and the yards in this development were about a quarter to a half-acre, which left him plenty of places to hide. Still holding the dog, I took my free hand, raised my index finger, and began a scan of the yard. I located her husband hiding behind a tree. He would not show himself.

Next, I was suddenly back in the house running for the front door. I felt myself inside her body, heart racing and frantic. There was a flash. I stared straight at her ex-husband who had managed to get inside the foyer. Though she had locked herself in the living room behind the double doors that separated it from the foyer, he had smashed them open with his feet and gotten in. I saw him standing just inside the doorway, holding a plunger. His intention was to beat her with the handle.

I was still inside her body, and we were running for her life towards the doors to get out of the living room and to the front exit. It was too late. I saw blood on the doors in the foyer. We didn't make it out.

I awakened shaking and annoyed. *Dang it! What had happened? Why didn't she listen to me?*

During my next mentoring session, I immediately described the dream, explaining that I was unable to save this woman.

My mentor said, "Your guides wanted you to have this experience, where you were unable to help, to show you that you are the messenger. Everyone has free will and, if they choose not to listen to you, well, then, you know you tried and you have to move on."

Okay, lesson learned. Damn it!

Chapter Twenty-Seven
The Jeep Ride

The jeep was speeding up a snowy mountain road rather fast. As it rounded a bend in the road, it slowed down because a sheriff's car sat on the shoulder waiting for speeders. As we passed the sheriff, I noticed his cruiser had a body style out of the late 1970s or early 1980s. A metal mounting bar was attached to the top to hold the flashing lights.

As I sat in the front seat, I felt like I was inside someone else's body again. I looked over and saw a man with dark brown, tussled hair and a mustache driving the jeep. I didn't have a good feeling about what was about to occur. As in the case of the woman who was beaten with the plunger, I knew this man driving the jeep was not going to listen to my advice.

We arrived at a restaurant that overlooked a mountain that faced a wall of trees. Instantly, we found ourselves inside the restaurant. I was still in the body of the jeep passenger, who was a good friend of the driver. As I scanned the crowded restaurant, I looked for the likeliest person who might present a problem in this scenario. I said to myself, "No, it's no one in this room."

I told the man driving the jeep, "We need to get our food to go and eat it down the mountain a bit. I feel like there's going to be an issue with someone here."

The jeep driver just looked at me with exasperation, and we headed over to order the food to go. Holding the to-go boxes, we walked toward another door that led outside, going through a side dining area on our way out. The driver put his box of food down on a small table as he considered whether what I recommended was really what he wanted to do. I quickly turned to gaze towards the back of the small dining area where there was a room with a pool table. As I looked closer, I spotted a young man in his twenties wearing a white button-down polo shirt. He was pushing another young man back into a corner and yelling in his face as he banged his finger on the other man's chest. The young man he was pushing yelled, "See, this is why I don't take you anywhere!"

I immediately said to the man who was driving the jeep, "There! Right there is going to be your problem!" He glanced over and saw what was happening in the pool table room, and we both exited the restaurant with our to-go boxes.

As we approached the jeep, the man whose body I was in got in, but the driver did not. Instead, he said, "I want to eat my food right here!" He proceeded to stand just outside the vehicle to soak up the beautiful scenery. He opened his food container and started eating. Just then, out of nowhere the man in the white polo shirt appeared. He ran up behind the jeep driver and hit him so hard in the back of the head that his body bent completely in half. I saw the whole thing and my heart sank. The jeep driver seemed to straighten his body, looked right at me, and said, "Well, you were right and now I'm dead." It was, of course, his spirit that spoke to me. I could see right through him.

I was still inside the body of his friend who was in a state of panic. Internally, I said to him, "We have to get out of here!"

He frantically started looking for the keys to the jeep, which I saw hanging on the turn signal indicator. I told him where the keys were, and he grabbed them and tried to figure out which key would start the jeep. His hands were trembling, and we were losing precious time.

I said, "Slow down and go key by key, and I will tell you which one will start the engine."

He began to show me the keys one by one, and soon I saw the ignition key. I told him to start the jeep but that he needed to crouch down behind the steering wheel. I knew that as soon as the man in the white polo shirt heard the engine turn over, he was going to make a beeline for the jeep and do the same to this man as he had done to the jeep driver.

We crouched down, started the engine, quickly pulled out, and headed towards the sheriff we saw on the road earlier to try and get some help. Bang! I was awake.

My mentor later explained that I was able to save the man whose body I had occupied. She further explained that the man in the white polo shirt went on a rampage after killing the jeep driver because he was out of control. She said the jeep driver was not the only one hurt that day. I am unsure if anyone else was killed.

Chapter Twenty-Eight
Kauai

"I really want to go to Hawaii," I said to my mentor. "I went once in the 1980s to Maui, but I want to go back. I can't help it; it's all I can think about lately. I feel like I need to get there so I can get back—if that makes any sense."

My mentor said, "Well, you're going home."

Huh? I asked what she meant, and she replied by describing the continent named Lemuria or Mu that existed thousands of years ago. It was older than Atlantis and was believed to be the home of some of the first humans on Earth. She further explained that the Pleiadians were the beings who seeded humanity and, therefore, my urge to visit Hawaii was a homecoming for me since most likely I had my first lifetime on Earth there. I had been looking for information on trips to Kauai, and, just as I was about to share that with her, she said, "In particular, you should visit Kauai."

As soon as we hung up, I was on the phone again, this time, with my daughter. "We *have* to go to Kauai," I said.

She replied, "Okay, Mom! When?"

"As soon as possible," I answered.

A few days later, she made the one-hour drive from Houston to my apartment on the coast, and we sat in front of the computer booking airline tickets and reserving a one-bedroom condominium.

"What's the rush, Mom?" she asked.

"I don't know exactly, but I feel the time to go is now."

She shrugged and we went to bed.

We spent the next few days together talking about the things that were happening for me and she listened graciously. Her days of wondering if I was just "going through a stage" were finally giving way to the realization that just maybe the dreams I was describing could actually be true.

A friend and her husband generously agreed to drive me the hour and twenty minutes to the airport a couple of weeks later. They also were willing to look after my precious Larry for the eleven days I would be gone.

With butterflies in my stomach, I was filled with anticipation for what the trip had in store for us. I arrived at the airport and looked around for my daughter. She soon texted me from her phone and said she had arrived and was searching for me as well. We finally found each other, checked our bags, and headed for the gate to catch the first of our two flights. The first leg of the journey was to Los Angeles, and then we caught a direct flight from there to Kauai.

As we approached Hawaii after an uneventful flight, we were both glued to the tiny windows trying to catch a glimpse of the islands. As we searched the water below, we saw majestic green mountainous islands poking up out of the Pacific Ocean. We looked at each other in hopeful delight of what was to come.

After landing, we went through a long screening process with our covid tests and vaccination documents. Eventually, we walked outside and immediately felt the warm, inviting Hawaiian air. We hadn't made plans for transportation, so we called a cab and sat down to await their arrival.

After the cab arrived, we told the driver where we were staying in order to meet the required three-day quarantine at an approved hotel. My daughter and I were both quiet during the drive other than a few questions the cab driver asked us about our departure point. As I stared out the open window and felt the breeze gently blow across my face, I slowly closed my eyes and connected with the energy of the land and sea. Instead of seeing Kauai as it was now, I could recall how it looked countless centuries ago when it was an entire continent. It was as if the timeline was turning back. The highway disappeared, the buildings faded, and I was no longer riding in a cab. Yes, I could see it now! Images of myself existing in a peaceful village on the turquoise waters flooded my mind. There was no strife. I recalled the most amazing, peaceful coexistence and cooperation among the people who lived as one with each other and the land. I saw myself with a basket in my arms smiling as I walked barefoot on the orange sand that lined the beach. As the images came rushing back, a feeling of complete bliss overtook me. Minutes later, my eyes fluttered open, and, as we sped down the road, I saw the lush, emerald green mountains to one side and the deep crystal blue water of the Pacific Ocean on the other. I could feel a welling of emotions begin to rise. A guttural desire to cry was difficult to hold back. Just then the driver announced that we were about to arrive, and I drew myself back to the logistical issues of checking in and getting settled.

My daughter and I were traveling on a budget, so we ate a fancy dinner in our room that night and then called a grocery delivery service to have food delivered that we could prepare ourselves for the remaining days.

We were allowed to walk the grounds and swim in any of the three pools. A small bar and grill looked over the beach, but we were not permitted to go onto the seashore until the three-day quarantine was over. Restless, we spent our days at the pool just outside our room, taking walks around the grounds, and, of course, sitting in chairs that looked down on the beach we were dying to visit. Each morning my daughter and I were greeted by a colorful rooster crowing just outside the sliding glass door that led from our room to the pool and garden area. My daughter named him Henry. During our three-day stay, we became fast friends with Henry as he followed us around the grounds of the hotel.

Finally, day four arrived and we were cleared to leave quarantine with a negative covid test. We took a cab to a car rental place named "Rent a Wreck." (We were really on a budget!) We had reserved a small Toyota model that wasn't even manufactured anymore and was a stick shift. Luckily, we both knew how to drive a manual car, so that was not a problem, and the gas tank was full. After opening the trunk to put our bags inside, it wouldn't shut. Laughing at our little jalopy, we slammed the trunk a few times until it finally closed and walked over to open the doors whose squeaky hinges squealed in protest. We laughed again and hopped in, put the car in gear, and headed to the grocery store to get food for the condo.

Giggling all the way to the grocery store in the little white car (the speedometer stopped working as well), we were in the best mood now that we could move freely around the island. Grocery shopping out of the way, we took off for the condo. After arriving, I headed straight past the bedroom and kitchen and on through the living room to the patio doors dead ahead. Sliding the door open, I walked outside to hear the deafening waves of the Pacific crashing onto the shore as the sun was setting.

Tears streamed down my face. I had no words. Goosebumps covered my arms, and I felt as if I would fall to my knees. I was in awe and felt enormous waves of gratitude and nostalgia overtaking my body. This was as close to a true spiritual experience as I had ever known.

My daughter looked at me and said, "Mom, are you okay? You can't stop crying."

I replied, "I know I can't and I'm just going to let my tears keep falling."

After what felt like an hour, I gathered myself and headed back inside to unload the groceries and unpack my clothes. The condo was perfect, and the roar of the waves crashing could be heard even with the glass door shut, but we kept it open most of the time. Later, we piled into the king-sized bed we were sharing during our visit and fell fast asleep.

The next morning, we headed out to go on a hike. We climbed over 700 feet. When we reached a lookout point, we could see the "Sleeping Giant" mountain in the distance and just sat and got quiet as we soaked in where we were.

"It's just so beautiful, Mom," my daughter said.

"I know," I replied. For my daughter and me, this was a spiritual experience, and that nuance did not pass us by.

On another day, we took the rental car on a drive to the northern part of the island. We had no real plans and were content to just see where the day took us. As the little car climbed a particularly steep part of a cliff, the traffic stopped ahead because a boulder had tumbled down and blocked the road. We waited for a bit to see if they could clear it but after a while decided to turn around and take a different route.

We made our way back down and turned just slightly inland. We came upon a small town named Hanalei. It was tiny yet majestic and, as I slowly drove through, I saw a small green church off to the side that had amazing stained-glass windows. My daughter was startled when I pulled on the steering wheel sharply and cut over to park the car. We now faced the church.

My daughter asked, "What's up, Mom?"

"Just a feeling," I replied.

I didn't exactly know why we were sitting in the car staring at this church, but we lingered there for some time. When I had seen enough, I slowly put the car in gear and got back on the road. It was getting late in the day, and we decided to head back to Kaap'a to do a little shopping near our condo. As we walked down the sidewalk peering into store windows and deciding which ones we wanted to enter, we looked over and saw a sign outside one shop that said, "Everything 50% off. Going out of business." That sounded exactly like the budget we were working with, so we went inside.

We looked around for about thirty minutes. Just before I left the back of the store, I noticed a small box with watercolor greeting cards inside. I started combing through the cards and reached the back of the box, where a watercolor card with the green church we visited appeared near the end of the selections. I quickly pulled it out of the box and went over to my daughter and held it up. "Look!" I exclaimed.

"Oh, wow, Mom! That's the church we just came from."

"Yeah, I know. I'm going to buy it."

When I got home to Texas, I had a picture my daughter had taken that day of the green church and the watercolor card framed. They now sit right near me on a table by the couch. They are the first thing I see when I get home. Each time I look at them, I am reminded of that magical day and my heart warms.

Another day, we went whale watching on a boat with a few other tourists, two crewmen, and the captain. It was a barefoot cruise, so we took our shoes off before getting on the boat, then headed out to the Pacific to try and see some whales. When we came to a stop where one whale was sighted, I stood up and looked around at the deep blue water that surrounded us. Just at that moment the captain of the ship came up to the top deck as well. He took one look at me and started walking toward me. I could sense him coming to ask me questions, and I could plainly feel his curiosity. My daughter stood by uncomfortably as he asked, "So what is your story?"

What I wanted to say was, "Well, thousands of years ago, I came to this part of Earth and lived among the first humans. I know this land and these waters deep in my DNA, and this is a homecoming for me, so I'm taking in as much as I possibly can while I'm here."

Ultimately, I said, "Oh, I just left my husband of thirteen years, and I went away to kind of regroup and get myself together."

He had a kindness about him. He gave me some friendly advice about getting over tough times and shared how he had once been married to someone he should not have been; he also had left his spouse, and now all was well in his life.

On some level, I think he knew there was more to my story, however, because he kept giving me curious glances here and there. We would stare just for a moment at one another. He came and sat next to me for a few minutes as well, not saying anything, like he knew something was left unsaid but was too polite to ask. An hour later, without much luck sighting whales, we pulled back into the dock. As my daughter and I headed off the boat, he touched my arm and kindly said, "Just remember, things always get better eventually."

Over the rest of our time in Kauai, we did several other activities including a "no door" helicopter ride. We were both ready to get off 10 minutes after we left the ground.

The last day brought a trip to a locals' beach called Salt Pond. It was near the southwest side of the island and was low key with only a few tourists.

When first entering the parking area, we noticed a large group of tents where "houseless" people lived. "Houseless" is the term the inhabitants of Kauai used because these people had a home, just not a traditional one, allowing those without a typical residence the respect they were due. We drove farther down and found a place to park. We got out our chairs and cooler filled with lunch and drinks and settled into a spot.

To our right was a Hawaiian man with four small children who called him Grandpa. As we sat sunning in our chairs, listening to the Hawaiian children play in the shallow water, we watched as a couple of fat seals rolled over on the sand. I got a deeply calm and cozy feeling about that beach. Something just felt right. There was a barrier of volcanic rock that made a great pool for my daughter and me to swim in the cold water, which felt great on our hot skin. After several hours we decided to head back to the condo and get packed for our journey home to Texas the next day. We gathered our picnic and chairs and loaded them into the little white car.

I lingered on the beach for just a moment, memorizing what I saw. Months later, I would tell my daughter, "When I die, take my ashes to Salt Pond Beach and scatter them in the water."

Chapter Twenty-Nine
Not Your Husband

I stood in a futuristic house. I could not tell exactly what year it was, but the home looked like it was right out of a sci-fi movie. The walls were mostly floor-to-ceiling windows. The exterior was made of steel and glass. The interior décor was all black, white, and gray and felt sterile. A man was lying on the bed. He was not feeling well. I grabbed a nearby blanket and put it over him.

Then time went back a few hours. I walked up the hallway and entered the kitchen. I saw what felt like my husband looking for something to eat in the refrigerator and asked him, "Are you feeling okay?"

This dream was over rather quickly, and I wondered who this man was and what happened.

During the next session I had with my mentor, I got clarification that he was not my husband, but I acted as if I were his wife in order to call the EMS because he had a heart attack while his actual wife was away. I was delighted that I could help, and it gave me a glimpse of what houses would look like in the future as well.

Chapter Thirty
Devil's Tower

Later that same night, I dreamt I was in a small car headed up the coast in Australia. I was driving and my husband was in the passenger seat. It was the 1970s and I had long blonde hair and wore a green mini dress with white flowers. My husband also had blonde hair, and we were smiling as we drove up the coast together.

Suddenly, I could not see the road because there was nothing in my vision except the color green. In the middle of the swirling green color was an hourglass that was turning in a clockwise motion. I quickly pulled over and said, "I asked them not to do that while I'm driving!"

After several minutes on the side of the road, I pulled back out and headed for a local bar to stop and get a drink. My husband and I walked in and ordered, but there were no other customers. The bar was basically empty. The walls were mostly glass and looked out over the ocean on two sides. We were laughing, hugging, kissing, and generally having a good time by ourselves.

Flat screen TVs, which were not around in the 1970s, hung on the wall behind my husband. Two of them were facing right towards me. I glanced over at one of the TVs and saw a picture of Devils Tower, the mountain featured in the movie *Close Encounters of the Third Kind*. The other television showed an entire city that was rotating at an angle in a circle on its tectonic plate. I stared at each screen, not knowing exactly what I was seeing.

Again, I later consulted with my mentor, and she told me this was a message from my guides showing me that I had premonition abilities. She continued by saying that the city I saw turning on its tectonic plates was a premonition of an earthquake. It looked like a city near Kilimanjaro. She then asked if I could tell what year it was.

I answered, "2035."

She said, "Okay, then we'll wait till 2035 and see what happens." She went on tell me that some of the other dreams I was having concerning crimes were predictive and would occur in the future. She said it was like the movie *Minority Report* in which the oracles could see crimes before they were committed, and the police could be alerted to intercept before the crime was carried out.

This was a little alarming to me since the police would automatically be suspicious of my prior knowledge of a crime. I decided not to get too concerned, however, and leave it up to God and my spirit guides as to how all that would unfold.

A few weeks later, I was on a walk with Larry, and I heard the word "oracle" several times. When we got back to the apartment, I jumped on the computer and started doing research. A few minutes into my research, I came across a pre-Raphaelite painting of an oracle sitting atop a tripod chair as oracles of Delphi were known to do. I started crying and got goosebumps. I left the computer, went and sat down on my couch, and stared out the glass door.

Over the past few weeks, I had felt Atlas around me as well. In Greek mythology, Atlas was one of the Titans who led a rebellion against Zeus. As a result, he was forced to hold up the heavens for eternity. I spent several days trying to put together the signals I was getting about my identity in previous lives. It was a little too much to try to figure out on my own, so I wrote my thoughts down in my notebook to discuss with my mentor on our next call.

That session began immediately with me describing hearing the word "oracle" repeatedly and having the feeling that Atlas was reaching out to me. She verified that indeed I was one of the oracles of Delphi. Her angels also told her that Atlas was my father. Now, I had a better understanding of how I was able to give predictions and premonitions because I had done it in other lifetimes, so this was an ability I only had to bring out of the closet again.

Chapter Thirty-One
Leaving Texas

Late summer of 2021, I heard a knock at my door. Though I had changed my phone number months earlier, my ex-husband was at my apartment. He was a mess and had been evicted from his home. He was hoping to stay with me, but I declined. This proved to be a point of contention with him, and he proceeded to make my life miserable.

Exhausted from trying to avoid him in a small town over the previous year, I decided it was time to leave Texas. I was ready for a fresh start in a new environment where no one knew me and I could grow into my abilities without distractions. Near the end of August, my daughter and I headed east in search of a new home.

As we made our way across the country, I fell into periods of deep depression, feeling insecure and anxious about my decision to leave the only life I had ever known and everything familiar behind. I became overwhelmed and second guessed my decision to relocate. As the days progressed, I started experiencing several episodes of déjà vu each day. Then my daughter began having the same thing happen to her several times in a single day. This continued for a few weeks until we finally landed on the apartment that I was to settle in. I learned from my mentor that my guides were sending us these episodes of déjà vu, or glimpses into my future, in order to calm my misgivings and show that we were on the right path.

I am blessed to have the daughter I have and couldn't have made this frightening move without her. I came through one of the toughest times in my life thanks to my daughter's can-do attitude and loving support. My mother, stepfather, and the father of my children also supported me, both emotionally and financially, to help make the transition to somewhere I could feel safe and flourish. We had come a long way as a family over the years, and when the chips were down they came to my aid. I will always be grateful for all their love and encouragement.

A couple of weeks after unpacking and settling in, my daughter boarded a plane headed back to Texas. It was official now. I was on my own for the first time in my life. No family and no significant other. Just me and my guides moving forward into the unknown. I had no sense of what to expect. I prayed for guidance and did my best to remain open to receiving it.

I had recently been introduced to a friend of my mentor who had plans to open a crystal shop in late fall 2021 in a town near my new apartment. I met the owner over lunch one afternoon, and it was decided I would manage the shop once we prepared it for the opening. It has been a delight acclimating to my new home and working at the crystal store. The energy is light and expansive. It infuses me with anticipation about my life moving forward, and I am filled with a sense that this is where I will flourish. The shop owner and my co-workers are a wonderful new soul group that support me in my endeavors to develop my gifts. Quietly encouraging, they have listened as I have described my gifts and what I see for my future. They each have their own unfolding journey, and it is with joy that I watch them grow as well. I could not have asked for a better opportunity for growth and friendship. I pray that each of them knows how much they have contributed to my confidence and feeling accepted for who I am.

Chapter Thirty-Two
Yearbook of Ascended Masters

Since arriving at my new home in the fall of 2021, I have gotten comfortable with who I am and how my life is unfolding. I have started giving a few readings myself and become more confident about finding some of my own answers through the constant guidance of my beloved spirit guides. The dreams keep coming. Though I don't meet with my mentor as often as I once did, we are still in touch for dream interpretations via email and an occasional facetime meeting.

I recently sent a dream interpretation request to my mentor, telling her I had seen what looked like a page out of a yearbook of ascended masters with a blank spot in the middle of the page. Ascended masters are beings that have incarnated on Earth and have reached a level of enlightenment. They now assist humanity from higher dimensions. Lovingly, they guide and support where needed. Jesus, Buddha, and various saints and sages are examples of ascended masters.

My mentor explained that the yearbook I saw was *my* yearbook, and the ascended masters' pictures who were on that page were those I had worked with over my many lifetimes on Earth. She further explained that the blank spot on the page was for an ascended master that would be showing up to work with me on the premonitions I had been seeing of late. These intuitions concern the coming dismantling of earthly structures that no longer serve humanity going forward. She indicated that the ascended master I had not yet worked with felt like Mother Theresa and was coming forward to solidify my understanding of these premonitions so that I would feel confident in my visions. She encouraged me to be open to receiving her guidance. I look forward to doing just that.

I wait with anticipation for what this year, 2022, will bring for me and all of us here on Earth. I have invested a great deal of time and energy on this beloved planet, but my journey is not over. There is much left for me to do. God, my higher self, and my guides know what is next. I am not fighting anymore. Instead, I am going with the flow and feeling what is right and good. I am grateful for all I have and to all the people and beings that help me on this journey. I look forward to watching the rest of my life unfold with pleasure. I have only to listen to my intuition to know what is right and which way to turn when there is a fork in the road. I hope to spread wisdom, knowledge, and unconditional love during all my remaining years. I believe my teacher role will be coming in the near future, and I wait for guidance on how to proceed with that as well.

Healing is my purpose. I have always been a healer. It is a natural state for me to heal. It comes from deep down inside my DNA and is intrinsic to who I am.

As I walk through the rest of this life, I see it for all the beauty it holds. I have a feeling of contentment and knowing that all is as it should be. I await further instructions and dutifully carry on. I am finally at peace with myself and in awe of how well the Universe takes care of me. Each and every night, I thank God for my life and assure him I will show up again the next day to continue this grand finale of all the lifetimes I have spent here on Earth. I pray I did well across the many lives I have lived and that I can finish these lifetimes by knowing I did the best I could.

Thank you, Creator, for all you do for me and all the beings in the Cosmos.

Loving you always, Melina

www.ingramcontent.com/pod-product-compliance
Lightning Source LLC
Chambersburg PA
CBHW050442010526
44118CB00013B/1651